Amy Ninette – My Sister With Down Syndrome

Deanne Shead

PublishAmerica

Baltimore

First printing

ISBN: 1-4137-0982-6
PUBLISHED BY PUBLISHAMERICA, LLLP
www.publishamerica.com
Baltimore

Printed in the United States of America

For Mom and Dad,
Emily and Ethan.

Acknowledgements:

Many thanks to Denis and Melanie Keyes for their many hours of support, input, creativity, and help. They have been a very big help in my life and Amy's. I am truly grateful.

I have written this book describing what it was like to grow up with a sibling that has Down Syndrome. She had a tremendous impact on my life and many others.

I am now a mother of two and know what it is like to have fears or apprehensions of having a child with a disability. I think my book will help many realize it is very possible for children with Down Syndrome to lead "normal" lives.

PART ONE
ABOUT AMY

⌘ ⌘ ⌘ ⌘

CHAPTER ONE
LITTLE SISTERS

I wish I could say I remember every moment I spent with her, but life's memories don't work that way. You live your life day by day and every once in awhile something happens that makes you say "remember when?" What I can remember from when I was a little girl was having a little sister that sometimes got on your nerves, sometimes took your favorite clothes, toys, and the limelight of being the first child, the first grandchild. Despite all this, I grew to love my little sister Kendra. We learned to play together and sometimes fight together. And just when I was starting to get used to one little sister, another one came along. Now there are two – two to take your toys, and two to share everything with. You might as well say it, 'cause when it comes down to it, "you're the oldest, and you know better," and that's just how it's going to be.

But what if the youngest sister was *different*? What if she required special needs? What if she had *Down Syndrome*?

Her name was Amy – Amy Ninette. She was all of the above, and then some. And she was my baby sister. My baby sister, who taught me more about life than any sister can, any person can, or any book can. I learned patience, understanding, appreciation, strength, and determination, but most of all, about family, a special bond, never to be broken, held together through it all.

To this day I don't know what my parents said to Kendra and me when they first brought Amy home. It was August, 1975. Our birthdays were in November. Kendra would be two years old, and I would be four. But we accepted her, and we loved her. She was our little doll, most often referred to as the "little bird." I guess many thought she looked like a little bird. She seemed very tiny, delicate. What we didn't know was how delicate she really was. At birth she weighed 6 pounds, 3 ounces. Amy spent several months in the hospital, struggling with pneumonia. When she was a month old, her weight had dropped to 5 pounds, 14 ounces. At three months, she had made it to 10 pounds, but lost a pound in just one week due to her illness. I will always remember my mom saying how close we came to losing her those first couple months of her life.

"She was a very sick little girl," she'd say.

But she overcame those battles. Little did we know this was only the beginning of a lifetime of battles.

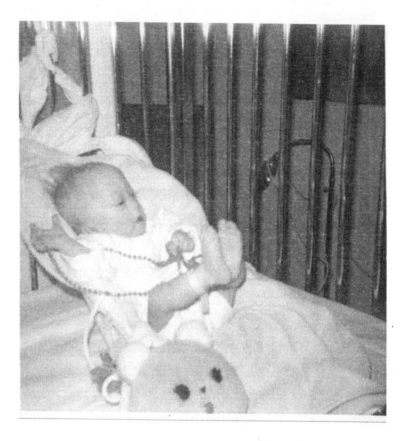

Amy in the hospital at 3 months old.

What does a parent think when they are told their child has Down Syndrome? My mother, Lois Tucker, has told me about her feelings those first few days she had Amy home from the hospital. I think she knew from the moment she brought Amy home that something was different about her. The more she looked at her, the more convinced she became. My father, Spencer Tucker, well I haven't heard him speak of those days very much. He's the kind of person that just goes with the flow. And when it's time for him to speak, everybody listens.

Would you believe me if I told you the doctors sent Amy home with a clean bill of health and no signs of Downs? It was only because my mother had insisted on further testing and exams that we soon found out she had all the characteristics of a child with Downs. She had short little fingers and toes, her eyes were different and her ears weren't fully developed, and her tongue was slightly larger than normal. She also seemed to be missing her sternum. Her chest almost looked concave. But that didn't mean she wasn't a beautiful little baby. She was still a miracle, a wonderful creation, and no one was going to tell my parents any different. Their beliefs and their concerns may not have been clear to me at the tender age of four, but I certainly knew they loved her. We all loved her. This concluded our family of five.

My family heard several questions including: "What are you going to do with her?" "Will you put her in an institution or a home?" "How will she walk or talk, or feed herself?" "This little girl is going to change your life drastically."

Little did they know. This little girl would not only become the center of our immediate family, but she would become the highlight of our whole family. She would touch the lives of everyone she met. She would leave an imprint on every person she touched. And she would become a little girl who could capture your heart, take your deepest emotions and read them without even trying, and react in a way that only a genius could. I have often wondered, how can someone with so many problems – what some might call a *handicap* – be so perceptive, so sensitive and so unique?

Amy

CHAPTER TWO
A HOME IN THE COUNTRY

When I was five my parents decided a home in the country would be a more ideal place to raise three girls. So, from the big city of Peterborough, Ontario, often referred to as "Peterpatch," we moved to the little subdivision called Mallard Bay on Pigeon Lake. On a good day, it was a twenty-minute drive from Mallard Bay to Peterborough. It was a small subdivision with good people, and like most small subdivisions or towns, everybody knew everybody. It wasn't long before we got to know all the neighborhood kids, and their pets.

The house in that little subdivision was well-known. We've always had an "open-door policy." It was a common scene to drop in on a weekend to find a house full of people. If they weren't sitting around the table in the tiny dining room they were rocking in the basement with a stand-in bartender – usually an uncle or close friend – and Spencer, my dad, playing his guitar. The Tucker household became a meeting spot for many. And if you wanted to hear a little jam session in progress, a Friday or Saturday was a good bet. Other family members and friends would join in, too. It was not unusual to have a banjo, a fiddle, harmonica, and a couple guitars, even a set of spoons, anything that made music. And Amy, she'd be right in the middle of it all. If nothing else my parents wanted her to experience everything she could. They wanted to include her in everything, especially our family.

We grew up doing everything little kids do. And Amy was always right there with us. Although it didn't happen right away, Amy did learn to ride a bike. Through the summer months we rode our bikes to the end of the road, the circle/dead end, and back. The starting point was always the McCormick house, basically the first house you met on the old dirt road going into Mallard Bay. It was also a great place to go. The McCormick's household included five kids. Once

Spencer on guitar, Amy playing the spoons

you rode past the McCormick's place it was a slow upgrade to a long downhill, followed by a soft curve to the right. Riding our bikes down this stretch was always fun. If you didn't make the soft curve to the right at the bottom of the hill, you'd head straight to the lake. There were always a slew of bugs that had flown up that trail. We weren't long learning to keep our mouths closed on the way down. If you got up enough speed you could make the turn and continue up the next small hill, past the first three houses to house number four, the Tucker's.

The main highway out to our subdivision was known as the "Yankee Line." From there you took the dirt road past the Frank's farm to the "T" in the road. The "T" is where Reno lived. Reno was an old horse that belonged to the Hickey family. He had foundered several years ago and was confined to the paddock in front of the barn where the green grass *doesn't* grow. We all spent many hours at that fence line whether we were waiting for the bus or just stopping by on one of our many bike rides. Being as kind as the Hickey family was, they didn't seem to mind. We would grow to know the Hickey family very well.

Our babysitter was Pam Hickey. She had a horse, too. His name was Cheyanne. I know I spent many hours watching for Pam and Cheyanne to come 'round the corner. She always had time to give each of us a ride. Amy looked forward to Pam coming to visit. She was a little bit scared and a little bit fascinated with Cheyanne, and she adored Pam. So when she came to baby-sit, it wasn't all that bad.

During our years at the elementary school, our bus would take a left at the "T" in the road and drive all the way down into Mallard Bay. It was very convenient or shall I go so far as to say we were a little spoiled. When we were kids, the bus picked us up at the end of our driveway, drove to the dead end, did the circle and came back. This also worked well for us. If we missed the bus the first time down the road we could catch it on the way back. But when high school rolled around we not only learned to grow up, we learned to walk. There's not enough room to do a circle and come back at the "T." Therefore, if we weren't there it wouldn't make the left turn to Mallard Bay. It took a right and continued on with the route.

What I haven't mentioned yet is the fact that it was approximately 1.5 miles to the "T" from Mallard Bay. Even further if you lived at the circle at the end of the road, like the Mannings' kids did. Need I mention again, we lived in Ontario, Canada? We experienced many a cold wintery day walking to the "T" to catch the bus. The road from the subdivision to the "T" was mostly farmland. In other words, lots of open space for wind to blow the snow across the road and to blow through our skin, thus making the walk to the bus stop a *wee bit chilly*.

The only plus that ever came from this dreary situation: the bus was cancelled on occasion. The snowplow may not have been down our roads yet, the drifts may have been too high, or better yet the dirt roads were too icy, making the bus driver stick to main roads only. And throughout all the years we lived in Mallard Bay, one child got her own personal driver to take her to school. She rode in a vehicle that was always warm and had a driver who loved her dearly. A driver who loved her like a granddaughter. A driver who became as special in her life as she was in his. That driver's name was Ted and that special child was Amy.

CHAPTER THREE
THE COTTAGE

The side of Pigeon Lake that we lived on wasn't known as a good place to swim. It's a very marshy, mucky, boggy lake. On top of that, there are several weeds. I'm not much on weeds. So most of our swimming took place at either the Hickey's pool or Grandma Helen's cottage. Approximately 30 minutes north east of Peterborough is a little town called Havelock. Just north of Havelock is Round Lake, our summer getaway. Trips to the cottage were always a treat. Not only because of the excitement of going there but the actual drive into the cottage was always the beginning of a fun weekend. The road leading to the cottage road was hill, after hill, after hill. My parents, or whoever happened to be driving, would speed up the hills and let off the gas for the downside thus creating a mini-roller coaster for whoever was in the back seat, and therefore, giving the back seat riders a stomach full of butterflies and giggles for miles. We renamed this road, the Wee Road.

The Wee Road led to the Cottage Road, which was always a neat road to drive on. The drive in to Grandma Helen's consisted of a bumpy one-lane dirt road with a couple of sharp turns and the odd small hill. Therefore, if you met someone on the way in, one of you had to back up to the next available driveway to allow the other to pass. The alternate choice, pull over to the right, into the edge of the woods and risk getting stuck, especially in the springtime.

On the left side of the road was a long row of cottages. Each had a front porch view of Round Lake and their own little beach or dock to swim from. Each cottage had its own unique little touches. One even had a tennis court, lakeside. What happens to the amateur's tennis balls? I bet that made an interesting underwater scene for the fish.

The woods belonged to my grandmother. It had been in the family for years. Her father tapped the trees every spring and had a *sugar shack* where he boiled the sap to make maple syrup. I still remember trekking through the snow in early spring back in the woods to the sugar shack to pack snow on a popsicle stick and dip it in the warm, fresh, maple syrup. It was a sweet treat on a cold winter day.

The sugar shack stood for years and years, and long after it was used for boiling the sap, it continued to create memories for us kids. We created a secret get-away there. It became a *criminal's hide-out* during the days we all played *Charlie's Angels*. We sometimes went back there just to reflect in the memories. You could almost smell the sap boiling, or picture "the days of yesteryear." It didn't matter what time of year it was. It was always a special trip back in the woods. In the fall, we would collect fallen leaves on the way back to the cottage. Grandma would always make her secret paste. We later found out it was only flour and water. That special paste worked well for pasting our beautiful leaves on the old fridge and in scrapbooks.

The only time going back in the woods was a problem was when one of us didn't come back. When the head count was one short, you could almost always bet on it being Amy. How she managed to fall behind or for us to lose sight of her was beyond our imaginations. She was very quick at disappearing. The *Grand Search* would commence usually involving almost everyone on our side of the lake. She was always found with either a neighbor or their pet(s). Strange as it was, Amy knew no enemies and no strangers. We all knew this was not always a good thing.

I'm not sure which season I liked the best. In the spring, the trees and flowers were blooming and the forest's bed was always covered with trilliums, the provincial flower. During the summer months, the trees and foliage were so rich and full that it covered the Cottage Road like a canopy. And in the fall, the canopy changed to the richest colors autumn has to offer. As fall progressed, the leaves fell to the ground creating a soft rain of reds, browns, yellows, and burnt orange.

It was very rare that we went to the cottage during the winter months, mostly because we would have to have a snowmobile to get there. The snowplow didn't make it to the Cottage Road. The other reason, probably the most obvious, there wasn't any running water, or insulation at the cottage and the only means of heat was a small wood stove which stood in the corner. On a chilly, damp, spring morning it was great to take the chill out of our bones. But it could never withstand the bitter cold January or February mornings. Therefore, Easter weekend signified the grand opening of the cottage for the summer months. And Thanksgiving weekend meant the end of another summer and the weekend to close everything up, including shutting the water off, and taking all the boats out of the lake, 'til next year.

Gone fishin'

We all loved the cottage, and Amy loved to swim. The cottage wasn't just a place to swim, it was a place for family get-togethers, summer regattas, hide-and-go seek, fishing, boat, canoe and paddle-boat rides, cards and bonfires, etc., etc., etc. To the right of the dock was a small sandy area, which was suitable for wading into and for us kids who were still learning to swim. It would be a common place for Amy. My dad used some rocks to create a small barrier to keep her from wading out to the big rock or deeper waters. And regardless of the fact that her swimming hole was only a foot to a foot and a half deep, she still wore a life jacket. Even when she got older and became a very good swimmer, she still liked to wear one at times. We never asked why.

CHAPTER FOUR
FIRST PETS

We always wanted a pet in the house. A dog was at the top of our list. As the years passed, we would come to learn that Amy had a special bond with pets. Please understand I'm not talking about just a simple love for them. And I'm not going to say she communicated with them either. It was simply *an understanding.*

I can always remember a dog in the house. A Dalmatian named Pepper who wasn't very friendly. We couldn't keep her for obvious reasons. Three small children in the house and several cousins close in age running around on a regular basis. An aggressive dog would never work. Then there was Sparky, a mutt, sometimes, the best kind. We were so young when we had Sparky. The only story I ever hear about him is the day Kendra was "calling" for him. She was very young, just starting to talk.

She was on a chair at the breakfast table, knocking on the window calling "Fuck-y, Fuck-y," or so it sounded.

My mom gets a kick out of that story. I've heard it told several times. And of course no one knows where she would have heard *that* word.

Like many kids, we brought home animals we felt were in need of sheltering. Those starving and totally helpless. Among the several kittens, puppies, birds, mice, and others, we had rabbits. I will never understand to this day what makes a child think that animals should go in places they don't belong or normally live. All part of the growing process I suppose. But what would make Kendra, at a very young age, feel that *my* bunny could swim? Not only could she swim, but that she should swim in the *toilet?* I have not so fond memories to this day of Daddy carrying my bunny by the ears, sopping wet, to its burial. And of course I hated my sister, or rather, I thought I did.

At some point in little girls' lives they feel this anger towards their sibling only to live another day and love one another again, possibly

Amy sitting, Standing – Kendra on left, Deanne on right

more. It's what sisters do. I must admit I felt this anger toward Kendra on several occasions. But can anyone explain why I may have felt anger toward Amy for only a second, if only a second, and then laugh? You learn to laugh. Not because she's different, but because that's all you can do when you're around her. You can't explain it, you just feel it. Holding a grudge toward Amy was impossible.

Our next pet was a toy poodle, Sammy. He was a pet to love and feed and for mom to clean up after. Yes, the reality of it all: Mom had to do the dirty work. Sammy lived a regular life. A life I thought was a happy one for him. We gave him love, played with him, and gave him the odd bath, a regular dog's life. I think being around us kids had its moments though. Every once in a while you need a break. All in all, from what I remember, he was a good little dog. He didn't wear bows and ribbons like many poodles, except for the odd time you may have found a doll's dress on him. And despite the fact that he was a little boy, he tolerated it and us.

CHAPTER FIVE
MOLSON

I'd like to say that this story happened a little differently, but it didn't. This is your typical "he followed me home" story. On one of our many trips home from the "T" in the road a dog followed us home. Actually, if I remember correctly, I saw him trotting along side the road as the bus drove past him. When I got off the bus, I waited. It was a dirt road with only two farms on it. He must be lost, or at least I hoped he was. He was a beautiful yellow lab with the kindest face. I decided I had to wait for this poor, lost dog, to of course take him home with me.

As he got closer and saw there was someone waiting for him, his expression changed from the face of a wandering dog to that of a dog that was on his way to meet someone he met every day. And I greeted him with open arms. Fortunately, because the walk home was a long one, I had plenty of time to think up my story of how this sweet, poor dog had "followed me home."

By the time I got home, we had been friends for life. He met Kendra and was surprised to see more than one happy child's face to lick and love on. When Amy got home, it was triple the fun. He was especially drawn to Amy. It was obvious to all that he had found a home he loved and a *special child* to watch over. And that's exactly what he did.

We decided our new friend needed a name. After a few hours of names like "Sport," "Rover," and "Bud," my dad had a thought. He once met a German Shepherd named "Molson" and he kind of liked the name. And only because he was a yellow/golden lab, we all thought it would be suitable to name him *Molson Golden*. It was a popular beer in our household and therefore everyone thought it was a cool name for such a *great* dog.

Being the kind and gentle dog he was, it was clear to all of us that this dog belonged to someone. His coat was beautiful. He was very obedient. Someone had obviously put in a lot of hours training him for hunting, and he had tattoos in both ears. My parents thought it would only be fair to try and locate his owner. We put ads in the newspaper and called in to a local radio show to see if his owners were looking for him. And of course every night my sisters and I wished we'd never find them.

After a couple weeks a phone call came through from a man who lived two subdivisions over from us, in a house way back off the main highway, the Yankee Line. You could only see the house from on top of one of the hills. He was very well known throughout the Peterborough area, as he owned one of the area's largest electronics stores. So much to our dismay, and to my parents dismay as well, though they may not have admitted it, Molson was actually Doc, and he had to go home.

Days went by of children moping, and parents wondering *when will they get over it, when will we get over it?* Until one day, a yellow dog came wandering back to Mallard Bay. The excitement of being reunited with our Molson lasted only hours though. My parents felt obligated to call his owner. After all, he must be missing this wonderful dog. So once again, we felt the pain and anguish of losing "our best friend."

It didn't end there though. Molson came back. He came back several times. Every time he got out or loose, he came straight to our house. Several times my dad would call his owner. Until one day, instead of my father calling him, a phone call came from Molson's owner. He asked if we would like to keep Doc.

"After all," he said, "he must be happier there. He goes there every chance he gets. I give up!"

And so "Doc" was no longer, and Molson it was!

Over the years Amy and Molson grew to be inseparable. He doted on her every move. She could do no wrong in his eyes. Everyone knows kids aren't easy on dogs, especially big ones they have no fear of. It's inevitable that tails get pulled, ears get tugged on, eyes get poked. I could add several more to the list, but I think you get the picture. Wherever the Tucker girls were, you could always find

Molson, usually at Amy's side.

There was only one time that anybody thought harm might come to Amy from Molson. And boy, were we delightfully surprised. My Grandma Cassidy happened to see Amy walk down the hill in the front yard toward the road. Keep in mind this is a small subdivision. There aren't many cars traveling up and down this road. Just as Amy went to step on the road, Molson grabbed her by the arm with that big old Labrador soft grip. He tugged softly to pull her back from the road. My grandmother couldn't get out there fast enough. Much to her surprise, Molson didn't even leave a scratch. Traffic or no traffic, he didn't want her on the road by herself.

Molson and Amy

CHAPTER SIX
SCHOOL

As expected, Amy's speech and learning skills weren't developing as fast as other kids. When she was seventeen months old, she was enrolled in a program at Five Counties Children's Center. One year she was featured on the front of their pamphlet. Special transportation had to be arranged to get Amy to school. They began working on her communication skills. We found sign language to be very helpful when she was starting to talk. Many Down Syndrome children have a tongue that is slightly larger, thus making it difficult to speak. Basic sign language helped both Amy and us. I could see the frustration in her face when she couldn't get her point across.

Signing became a big portion of Amy's communication skills, but we all continued to speak to her. Our family was rather large and also included a broad spectrum of friends. Thus, you can imagine we all had different personalities and shapes and sizes. For some strange reason, Amy was able to pinpoint a characteristic or gesture that would depict each person. It was always something so strong or vivid that it was very clear as to whom she was referring to. It was one sign and one sign only that portrayed each individual. I won't mention names as some signs may be considered somewhat embarrassing. Those who know their signs, sorry, but this is part of her that cannot go unmentioned, and I'll only mention a few.

On a simple note, her sign for her uncle, one of many who liked to tease, was the horns of a bull coming at you. It was just a simple game, much like The Claw to many kids. Of course she giggled with laughter every time he did his sign. Another uncle loved to mimic the old television commercial for Eat More chocolate bars. Remember Frankenstein crushing the chocolate bar in his forehead obviously not knowing where his mouth was and what it was for?

This uncle's sign: he'd make a fist and say the ever-popular word in our household, "EAT."

A friend of the family, and again, I'm not mentioning names, was sometimes caught picking his nose. Guess what his sign was? You can just imagine the response she got from us when she mimicked this particular friend. We probably weren't a good influence when she used this sign. Our reaction was rather elaborate. Our laughter made her chuckle her devious little laugh. She knew that was not a good sign. We have all heard the phrase – "fueling the fire."

A very close friend to the family sometimes referred to as our aunt, was a big help with reprimanding us kids. Her sign: her left hand on her hip and her right hand, index finger pointed, waving in a "don't sass me" motion. It was a popular scene in our house only because Amy was always teasing even when she was being scolded. And again, how do you keep a straight face? When do you draw the line and say that's enough? You can't get mad. Upset, possibly for a moment, but never for any length of time.

When Amy's skills continued to develop it was decided that she could move to regular school. She was five years old. My mother would insist that Amy be treated as any other child. She was placed in the Special Education class. It was a very diverse group of children. There were many different levels of skills and socialization. After a period of time, my parents noticed Amy was developing several bad habits – things that she wouldn't normally do. She seemed to be bored. She would hit herself when she was frustrated or mad. She didn't care for her personal hygiene as much as she used to. Of course my parents were very concerned. Everyone had worked so hard to keep her from doing such acts. It was clear that many of the children in her class were unable to control certain bodily functions or muscle spasms. And we knew Amy was not one of these children.

My parents fought to have her moved to a different classroom. Several letters and phone calls later they were able to convince everyone that Amy *should* be integrated into other classes.

CHAPTER SEVEN
THE LINE

Much like many children, we knew where *the line* was, and like many we tried to cross it. This is just one of the many situations where Amy was no different than the rest of us. Sometimes Amy's way wasn't the best way. Therefore, reprimanding was necessary. This usually involved the time-out method. It seemed to work the best with her as she hated being separated from us.

I will never forget the weekend my grandmother was babysitting us. Amy had done wrong, *crossed the line.* There was a slight flaw in the design of the bathroom cabinets. It didn't take long for Amy to figure out that once the door was closed all you had to do was open the drawer just inside the door and you could deny entry to all others. She found it very entertaining to have us in a panic, pleading for her to close the drawer. It was especially fun for her when one of us had to use the bathroom for its intended purpose, not as a playroom.

We had found a way to *break the lock* but we had to be quick about it. A letter opener or knitting needle could be used to stick through the crack in the door and by jamming it into the side of the drawer you could push the drawer closed inch by inch. The trick was to do it quietly, and when Amy wasn't looking. She was quick to pull the drawer open again if she caught on to what we were doing.

The weekend Grandma was visiting she decided it would be great fun to lock herself in the bathroom. She got into almost everything that could be gotten into, including my mother's makeup. When Grandma finally got in, there was lipstick everywhere. Amy knew she was in trouble. She must have really tested Grandma Cassidy's patience. We all know some grandmas tend to let the line go just a little bit farther. Grandma had marched her back to her room, Amy following hesitantly.

As the door was shut, the words "Fuck you Grandma" came from behind the door.

Those words must have ripped a hole in my grandmother's heart. I believe she chose to ignore that comment, and was probably right in doing so. Once again Amy had crossed the line with a giant leap I might add, and was forced to stay in her room just a few minutes longer.

You always tease the ones you love the most. This statement stands true in our family. But what happens if one goes too far? Is that possible? Amy was starting to cross the line with leaps and bounds. This of course became a big concern. She knew she was loved by all and was the center of attention on many occasions. But things were getting a little too mischievous. My parents agreed it was time to correct the problem. They turned to doctors and behavior therapists for advice. Their solution: to place Amy in a different environment. A family was chosen that included a married couple with two girls the same age as Kendra and me. Amy was eight years old. This family's home would become Amy's home away from home, the different environment. Amy would stay with them for two weeks at a time, thus allowing us to see her every other weekend. Not much time for a family to spend with the child that was the light of their daily lives, despite so- called "behavior problems."

Amy continued to go to school. Her behavior therapist would work with her both at home and at school. We all suffered through many months of visits from Amy, each visit being harder than the last. We grew to hate Sunday evening. Amy knew it better then any of us. And watching the tears swell up in her eyes was a heartache like no other. When the evening was approaching, she would go to her bedroom, put on her nightgown and close the door. I think she wished, just like the rest of us, that she could go to sleep in her own bed and wake up every morning in her own bed, walk to Mommy and Daddy's room and give them their good morning hugs.

As the months of glorious weekends and painful Sundays passed, we were noticing changes in Amy. I couldn't decide if they were changes for the better. When we went to pick her up, I was always expecting a warm, exciting "hello." But as time went on, she became a little withdrawn. I sometimes thought she was depressed. Were the Sunday evenings becoming too much for her? Did she hate us for exposing her to such pain? Like many, she was turning to food and watching hours of television in her time of sorrow. This was not our Amy. After almost a year, it was time for Amy to come *home*. That day hadn't come soon enough for us.

CHAPTER EIGHT
STRUGGLING FOR DEEP BREATHS

Year after year, Amy had regular visits to the doctor. She seemed to have a yearly cold with a touch of pneumonia. Tubes were placed in her ears at a very young age, no different than many young children. At the age of five, she had her tonsils removed. While undergoing this surgery, Amy developed keloid scarring from when the anesthetist had inserted the tube to intubate her for the surgery. A growth formed from the scarring that had to be removed. It had flopped over into her airway making it difficult for her to breathe. They had to give her a temporary tracheotomy, which she had for a week. They removed it before she was released from the hospital. Her breathing problems seemed to be getting progressively worse.

As the years passed, Amy was having more and more difficulty breathing, especially at night. We could hear her struggling for deep breaths. We would find her sleeping sitting up or propped up against a couple pillows. My parents were beginning to notice her fingers and lips were turning purple when she was lying down. She was a very ill little girl.

Once again my parents turned to doctors for help. We have several family members that work in the medical field. They all agreed it was necessary. So Amy was admitted.

Sleep studies at The Hospital for Sick Children in Toronto were performed on Amy at the age of ten. Amy was there for what seemed like ages. But she carried on. She never showed any fear and continued to be a happy child despite being away from her family once again. The doctors discovered Amy had come in to this world with a condition known as Trachea Malaysia. The rings of cartilage in her trachea/windpipe never fully developed. Every time she would lie down they would collapse, thus cutting off her oxygen supply. The only solution would be to give her a tracheotomy, which would more than likely be permanent.

This would begin a whole new world not only for Amy but the whole family. My parents wanted Amy to know exactly what was happening. They insisted that the doctors and nurses speak directly to her when giving instructions. She was highly capable of understanding the situation. After all, if someone told you "this would help you breathe," wouldn't you understand?

And so the Trache was placed and things changed. First and foremost, Amy could breathe at night. It must have felt wonderful to have a good night's sleep after such a long period of tossing, turning and waking up with a sore neck. She had to stay in the hospital for several weeks after the surgery was performed. There was a lot of adjusting to do. My parents had a lot of learning to do. It was like taking a first aid course in Trache care. My parents persevered, just another battle line to cross. And just like the previous battles, they were not about to give in. They pushed once again to give Amy a life that was as close to "normal" as they could possibly provide.

Weeks of changing, cleaning and replacing traches would pass. My parents had to become trache experts, as they needed to come home and teach as many family members as possible. They had been forewarned. Amy needed to have an experienced caretaker with her at all times. Throughout her stay in the hospital, Amy developed a friendship with many of the staff members and, of course, the other children in her room.

There are two children that stand out the most in my mind from Amy's stay at Sick Kids. One was a little boy who was approximately two years old. He had a rare disease and was quite ill. He was fed through a feeding tube in his stomach. He didn't have full use of his legs, he was deaf and blind and he, too, had a tracheotomy.

I really don't remember ever seeing his parents come to visit him. But I always remember how well he responded to Amy. A physical therapist had been working with him for several months. They worked with him daily on a mat on the floor at the hospital with little to no response. Amy would take him to his mat and play with him, clap her hands, "coo" at him, sometimes talk, what seemed like gibberish to most. And he loved every moment of it. He'd laugh and smile, and move his arms in excitement when Amy came across the room to visit him. The nurses always commented on how much of a response Amy would get from him. I think they were pleased to see him happy even if it was only for a few minutes. He was very ill and couldn't have been very comfortable for the better part of his stay at Sick Kids. It was always Amy he'd smile for. As with all the children at the hospital we could only hope he would get better and grow to live a happier life. We found out shortly after Amy left that he had passed away. His monitor failed to notify the hospital staff there was a blockage in his tracheotomy.

The other patient Amy shared her healing laughter and joking with was a young boy who had been involved in a very serious accident. Shortly after Amy had moved into her room in intensive care, a seriously injured boy was admitted. She went to him almost immediately. She always found a way to look into a person's feelings and open their hearts with strength and courage.

The boy had been riding his four-wheeler. A local farmer had given him permission to ride in his fields. He and a friend were out on what was considered familiar territory. When he was leaving the field to head for home, he didn't realize there was something blocking the opening to the road. What he didn't see was that the farmer had put a chain up across the entrance and as he passed through, it caught him. The chain hit him right at his throat level, and he was stripped from the four-wheeler and thrown into the ditch. His friend was able to stop before hitting the chain also and was able to run for help.

Aside from having scrapes and bruises, his lungs had begun to fill with blood. He had smashed his voice box and severed his jugular vein. If he had been alone, he may not have survived. Luckily his friend was able to get help, and he made it to the hospital for surgery and a long stay. He was brought into the room flat on his back with his head turned to the left side. They had made a special brace to keep his head in one position as he was not allowed to move his head during the healing process. Once again, Amy was drawn to someone in need.

She asked, "What happened?"

It was a very common phrase for her. And of course she wanted to help. So with the long days came many conversations and a friendship was built. Shortly after he became another friend in Amy's room, my father noticed the television was up on the wall to his right side, and he was facing the left. Dad got a mirror and put it up on the other wall so he could watch his favorite programs in the reflection.

Weeks passed and he was healing. The day for him to get up and to get out of bed had arrived. He had been bedridden for many weeks, and the doctors believed it was time for him to walk again. A wheelchair was brought to the room, and he sat down. His parents, the doctors, and relatives were all trying desperately to encourage him to walk with much dismay. Amy walked over, leaned down and spoke to him. There was something about Amy that radiated courage and strength. It wasn't in her words. It shone in her smile. He walked.

CHAPTER NINE
AMY COMES HOME

Going home was a day everyone anticipated, including my parents. For weeks, there were trips back and forth from Toronto to Peterborough and back again. Throughout it all, I'm sure my parents never had a good night's sleep. Going home was supposed to change all of that, but it was a "whole new ball game."

When Amy came home, she brought half of the hospital with her. There were three different machines that came with her, not to mention all the supplies. The first machine was designed to help keep the air entering her lungs from getting too dry. It blew a soft mist from a mask that was placed directly over the tracheotomy. Yes, yet another "thing" to go around what Amy had for a neck, which wasn't much.

The second machine needed an attachment, a new one with every use – a long catheter that had to be sterile as it was used to suction out excess fluids and mucous from her lungs. It was very thin in diameter but was several inches long. We had to insert it through the trache down her windpipe until it reached the bottom of her lungs. While withdrawing it, we had to go slowly and twist the catheter on the way up.

This was very difficult to get used to as it always made her choke and gag. Amy was always so good about it. If there were ever any difficulties with the "suctioning" process, she'd just take the catheter herself and say, "Let me try."

The third machine was the hardest to deal with. Just one more obstacle Amy learned to deal with in order to live at home and not in a hospital bed – her heart monitor. This machine had several wires with attachments and a large strap that had to go around her chest. What made this machine so difficult was the fact that any time she moved or the wires came loose, the alarm on the monitor would go off. What needs to be pointed out is that any time the heart monitor went off, everyone in the house thought Amy's heart had stopped or she wasn't getting enough oxygen. It was worse than any fire alarm. I remember jumping up from a deep sleep and running down the hall. We all felt the incredible urge to run to her bedside and make sure she was still breathing.

With all of these machines and supplies came several expenses. Ontario's health coverage only "covered" so much. And because my parents had been off work for several weeks already, I'm sure this wasn't easy. But they made it easy on us. Not once did we ever feel insecure or worried that there may be "other" problems. Looking back now, I'm sure this was not an easy task for my parents. But they managed. Fortunately they had to "manage" only for a little while.

What my parents didn't know was that they were about to find out how many friends they had, how good our "extended" family was to us, and what a community can do when they "pull together" for a family in need.

A benefit for "Amy and the Tucker Family" was organized. If I never had the opportunity to thank every person involved with this project, I'm doing it now. Whether they realized it or not, that benefit dance helped out our family more than anyone could know. This was an event that didn't just help my parents financially, it reminded all of us how important family and friends are. I'm sure my parents were deeply touched to know the lengths and efforts people will go to help people they care about.

PART TWO
AMY MOMENTS

⌘ ⌘ ⌘ ⌘

CHAPTER TEN
WITH A LITTLE HELP FROM AMY

Amy enjoyed helping out, whether we needed it or not. Through the years our house changed a few times. At one point, Kendra and I shared a room. Amy had her own. Then I moved to my own room and Kendra and Amy shared one. We shuffled around frequently. With each shuffle, there was always some remodeling. The only room that always stayed the same was my parents. From the dining room take a right and at the end of the hall was my parents' room.

Mom had decided to take down the old wallpaper in Amy's room and repaint it with a pastel green. She let us help take down the old paper and, as we all know, kids love to rip paper. The way we took the paper down off that wall you would think we were unwrapping a gift for ourselves. How ingenious of Mom to get a little help from her kids by giving them the pleasures of ripping down the old paper. The problem was that the paper didn't come down too easily. For as much as we loved to rip it, it was quite frustrating when only small pieces came off. So, our great imaginations kicked into overdrive.

We wanted to find a way to make it interesting. Our cousin Melanie was there for a visit and we put our heads together to come up with this: our closet was our spaceship. We climbed onto the top shelf in the closet, blasted off and landed on another planet. Our mission was to pull all the wallpaper down off of the planet. It kept us occupied for hours.

Between taking the old wallpaper down and painting her room green, somehow Amy found the paint. And, as always, it was one of these responses:

"I just turned my head for a second and look at her" or "where did she go?"

Well, this particular occasion had to be for a very long second because when we next looked at Amy, well she blended in with the wall. In that very long second, Amy had covered herself with green paint. My mother took her straight to the backyard, sat her down on some newspaper, and after taking a few pictures of her little "green Martian" daughter, she took the turpentine to her, For a brief moment, anger ran through my mother's mind and then, she laughed. Amy knew she had done a "no-no" and sat there with a grin from ear to ear.

CHAPTER ELEVEN
CABBAGE ROLLS

My mother was a great cook. The only thing she made that I didn't really care for was liver. But I didn't hold that against her, after all liver *is* liver and in my mind there isn't much you can do for liver to make it appealing.

Anyone who has ever taken the time to make cabbage rolls will know that this story may have made my mother cry, or at least come close to crying. If I remember the story correctly my mom had been slaving over the stove for most of the morning. She had finished cooking the meat, seasoning it, and had cooked the cabbage. She made pan number one ever so carefully; each roll was a masterpiece. The oven was preheating and she decided to put the first pan full of the delicately made rolls on the stove while she worked on pan number two.

Once again, she put every effort into the making of these difficult to wrap, delicious cabbage rolls. As she completed pan number two, she turned to place it on top of the stove alongside pan number one to prepare for the final touches. It may have been because she had worked ever so diligently on each of these pans that she did not notice that just because pan number two *was* pan number two didn't mean that there were *two* pans on the stove when she turned around.

So, there's only one pan on the stove. She must have wondered if she had possibly dreamt of making pan number one. Maybe she put pan number one in the oven already? But, much to her dismay, the oven was empty. I can only imagine the look on my mother's face when she opened the door to the basement. There sat Amy at the top of the stairs and Molson at the bottom. There was EMPTY pan number one on the floor in front of Amy. There was cabbage on every stair and I'm sure there was a smile on Molson's face at the end of the trail. Amy had fed him every last cabbage roll. How rude of him to not appreciate all of Mom's hard work! How inconsiderate of him to eat only the cooked, seasoned, still warm, meat!

We will never know whether Amy felt, 1) Molson was hungry, 2) she needed to feed him a "special" treat because of all the times she pulled his tail and tugged on his ears, or 3) if it was just to test my mother's patience.

CHAPTER TWELVE
AMY BEHIND THE WHEEL

Amy liked to mimic people. She did it very well – most times. Once in awhile she made mistakes. On this particular day she felt she could drive like "big" people can.

The driveway to the house in Mallard Bay went slightly uphill. Therefore, if the car was parked next to the house, the gear "reverse" was not always needed to get your vehicle to the road. One of Amy's favorite games was to lock herself in the car. She found great joy in watching us dance around the outside of the vehicle, begging or pleading with her to unlock the locks, or open a window.

Part of mimicking a person involves watching his or her every move. So walk through this with me: when a person gets in the vehicle, they sit down, shut the door, put on their seatbelt, turn on the car and put it in gear. Amy had been watching, studying, and observing, for many years. And so, Amy had chosen the day for *Amy* to drive. But add one more step to the routine – lock the doors before you start the car, so no one can interrupt you!

Now picture this: a little girl, only five years old, not tall enough to see over or through the steering wheel, let alone do a shoulder-check or look in the rear view mirror. Lock the doors, start the car and put it in reverse, see your family members running to the vehicle in hysterics with the look of terror in their eyes, giggle at them, and back out of the driveway.

The car she decided to drive was the new company car my father had just got, at his new job. What never ceases to amaze anyone that hears this story is the fact that at the precise moment the vehicle reached the road – Amy turned the steering wheel. If she hadn't, the car would have headed straight for Pigeon Lake. On the other side of the road, directly from our house, there were no cottages, and no obstacles. The only things that stood in her way were a beat up old fence and some bushes– undoubtedly no match for a vehicle in motion – with a hill to give it a head start.

CHAPTER THIRTEEN
ONLY THROUGH AMY'S EYES

My parents were always very concerned with Amy's emotions and ways of dealing with certain situations. Even in the saddest of moments, she always found a way to cheer us. Funny isn't it? We, being the older ones – are *supposedly* the ones who can handle the small crises, and the sad situations, but Amy was the one who always lightened the mood, gave us hope, and warmed us with her laughter.

Once again, my mother had wanted Amy to share in our sadness and understand the meaning of death, or the passing of a loved one. The first funeral Amy attended was for the father of our dear friend Dianne. He had not been in the best of health for many years. We all knew this day would be coming for Dianne's father, who was given the nickname "Blue."

Amy was sitting on the front porch of the funeral home after the service with Dianne, my mother and a nun with her habit on. They had been chatting for quite some time, catching up with the small town of "Tweed's" latest news and old friends. Amy sat quietly beside the nun watching her every move. After staring at the veil for several minutes, she slowly reached up and touched it. She then proceeded to touch the veil, and then touch her own hair, carefully comparing the two several times. My mother noticed her studying the nun's motions and gestures. But only when Amy finally decided to speak did she realize what Amy was so enthralled with.

Amy reached up slowly, touched the nun's veil once again and very innocently and quite honestly said, "I like your hair."

CHAPTER FOURTEEN
ONLY AMY COULD GET AWAY WITH THIS

We all seemed to trust Molson so much with our dear little Amy that he soon became her babysitter. Occasionally, he seemed to be her entertainer not her babysitter.

My mother was in the kitchen, and from the basement she could hear Amy giggling. It began as a tee-hee sort of giggle and soon turned into a giggle that went on and on, even some hysterical laughing. She soon realized that Amy must be either watching a great cartoon or something was up. She decided to investigate.

On her way down the stairs, she realized the television was not on. By the time she got to the bottom of the stairs she found Amy sitting in the middle of the floor with Molson stumbling in circles around her. Amy was getting great enjoyment out of his antics, and Mom realized she had come to his rescue. Amy had put one of his front feet through his collar and poor Molson was fumbling around on three legs.

I know it's probably not necessary to mention it, but I'm going to do it anyway. Even though Mom was Molson's hero that day, Amy was the one who received all the kisses when he was given his fourth leg back, despite the fact that *she* was the one who took it away from him, and proceeded to laugh at him to boot!

CHAPTER FIFTEEN
JUST BETWEEN SISTERS

Learning to drive in Canada meant learning to drive in all types of weather conditions. This usually involved a night or two in the K-Mart parking lot.

After a fresh snowfall was usually the best time to learn and the most fun to be had. The only way you can teach yourself to steer out of a skid or slide was to make it happen, and practice, practice, practice. And it was fun to "practice." Drive through an empty parking lot at a pretty good speed, turn the wheel and hit the brakes, now slide and steer. I know, I know, it's easy when you're in a wide-open space with no obstacles to hit, and you know it really doesn't matter which way you go. What a neat feeling. Why would you pay for a ride at the fair when you can spin, slide, slip, and do donuts in the K-Mart parking lot?

There's an enemy in this winter wonderland. It's called Black Ice and it has got to be one of the most feared road conditions a Canadian could ever encounter. You never know where it is, or when you're going to hit it. It sneaks up on you and can send you in whatever direction it pleases. Unfortunately, it lurks on highways and even sidewalks, and it seems like there's never a wide-open space when you need it.

So, you're sixteen years old, got your driver's license, and a '79 Chevy Nova to bomb around in. You've been driving for years it seems, most of them from your daddy's lap, but hey, you've got it down.

Winter was almost over; the snow was starting to melt. Kendra, Amy and I were on our way to the cottage in the Nova. My parents were already there and being the big sister with the driver's license, I said I would bring my two little sisters. It was one of those crisp afternoons when there's been sunshine for the better part of the day. It had melted some of the snow on the road to the cottage. That's right, the Wee Road. Throughout the day the sunshine was warm enough to melt the snow on the roads, leaving them wet, but easy to drive on. In the afternoons, when the sun started to go down, so did the temperature, making the wet, clear roads turn into a skating rink of black ice.

Kendra was in the front seat and Amy was in the back. As we approached the long turn to the right just before the Cottage Road, I hit it. I'm sorry to say that as I did, my hours of "practicing" in the K-Mart parking lot left me. I did exactly what any inexperienced driver does when they hit black ice. I hit the brakes. I'm not sure, but I may have hit them with both feet. The Nova did two complete 360s before it came to a stop. All three of us were screaming as we saw the road, the ditch, the road, the ditch, twice, and then came to a stop facing the right direction on the wrong side of the road. I turned to Kendra first, the look of terror slowly left her face and she turned a bright red with anger. My eyes then turned to the back seat.

As soon as Amy caught her breath and our eyes met – she smiled and said, "Don't ever do that again, Deanne!"

I had to giggle. Whether it was the warmth from her laughter or just the relief that we were all in one piece, I don't know. I took a few deep breaths and we continued on our way. Thank goodness there were no other vehicles on the road that day. I decided we were all okay so why tell Mom and Dad? Nothing happened to the car or us so I convinced my sisters to keep it between us.

Still a little shaken, we pulled in the driveway to the cottage.

I was the first in the door, not without saying before I entered, "Remember, we're okay, Mom and Dad don't need to know."

We marched in one after the other; Amy was the last through the door.

As she entered she belted out, "Deanne made the car go around and around and around, weeeeeeeeeeee!!!! It was funny!"

So much for keeping a secret – just between sisters. Amy wasn't good at keeping secrets.

CHAPTER SIXTEEN
AMY AND THE BULL

Behind the house in Mallard Bay there was an open field. Mr. Hickey kept his cows in there. On many occasions we would cut through the field to get to the McCormick's house or to go to my friend Krista's. Along the way we had to watch our step. Not only did we have to keep an eye out for the cows but we had to watch for cow manure as well.

Amy spent many hours playing in the backyard. With or without us, she found ways to keep herself occupied. Most of the time her faithful companion Molson was at her side. The backside of our house had windows looking into the backyard from every room. Thus making it easy for my mom to check on her whenever necessary. There were several things to keep her busy, a sandbox, three different-sized playhouses, toys, and at one point we had an aboveground pool that was filled with only enough water to wade in.

Like many children, she sometimes felt the need to explore. Amy also wanted to be like her big sisters and maybe that's why she decided it was time for her to cut through the field, too.

Once again, it only took a seconds for Amy to hop the fence and be face to face with one of Mr. Hickey's cows. Much to my mom's dismay it wasn't just any old cow. Amy chose the biggest cow in the field. My mother turned around just in time to find Amy looking into the eyes of 1,500 pounds of pure Limousine BULL. Her tiny, six-year-old, 45-pound body was no match for this bull. This is a true David and Goliath story. With not an ounce of fear, Amy marched up to that bull and popped him right on the nose. She then turned, climbed back over the fence, and continued on with her playtime, leaving the bull standing there dumbfounded! My parents were dumbfounded themselves at the simple fact that the bull did nothing, not a thing.

When my parents told Mr. Hickey the story, he, too, was

dumbfounded. The bull she so nonchalantly encountered was one of the worst bulls he had ever owned. He was one of the most difficult to deal with and most certainly was not one to allow someone to knock on his head. Especially someone he could have squashed without thinking twice about it, or give her a bunt strong enough to send her into orbit.

CHAPTER SEVENTEEN
BEWARE OF DOG

The bull wasn't the only neighborhood animal that Amy had no fear of. A young couple had moved in a few doors down from our house in Mallard Bay. Their names were Kym and Ian. They had a dog named Buster that had been teased and taunted by children as a pup. So, needless to say, this dog wasn't very good with children. Amy didn't know that, nor did she care. She was only five years old and had no idea that there was a sign on the property that said, "Beware of dog." If she did, she wouldn't have paid any attention to it. She knew no fear when it came to animals, she loved them all, and thought they all loved her. Perhaps that is why Buster became another animal on the list of pets that Amy shocked, surprised and had wrapped around her finger in no time.

Shortly after Kym and Ian moved in, Kym happened to look out her kitchen window just in time to see Amy walk into Buster's kennel/run. She had walked through the gate at the end of the driveway and straight to Buster. Knowing Buster's history with children, Kym ran outside expecting to find a crying child and a very upset Buster. But much to her surprise she found the two sitting together happily. Amy spoke to him as she pet him ever so gently, and Buster was relaxed enjoying the attention as though he had known her forever.

Calmly, Kym got Amy out of Buster's run and asked her where she lived. She walked her home and explained to my mother what had happened. After scolding Amy, Mom invited Kym in for coffee.

Before long Kym and Ian became regular visitors in our house. That was the beginning of a friendship that remains to this day. They referred to their pets as their children. Perhaps Amy filled that position, or was the closest they would get to having children of their own. She grew on them as she did with many. Her character, laugh and silly sense of humor were addictive.

Kym was Amy's worker and spent a great deal of time with her. The Association for Community Living had created a position to help children with Down Syndrome and disabilities get out in the community and enjoy social activities with supervision other than the child's parent. It gave Mom and Dad a bit of a break and gave Amy the opportunity to meet and spend time with new people, like Kym. Amy kept her on her toes, and they spoiled her rotten. And of course Amy soaked up every moment with them. Kym has a bubbly personality and Ian is more of the gentle giant type. However I describe them, they were great with all of us, and Amy loved them both dearly.

CHAPTER EIGHTEEN

I'M POPPA

Many evenings at the cottage were spent playing cards at the kitchen table. Our family enjoyed games like poker, euchre, bridge and cribbage, amongst many others. The kids played games like Croqinole, checkers, Snakes and Ladders, Cheat, and Nertz. Amy joined in whenever possible. If she wasn't interested she found other things to keep herself occupied. Much like any other seven or eight year old, she liked to dress up or pretend she was someone else. We all know she liked to mimic others and she was quick to learn their mannerisms. When Amy wanted your attention, most of the time she knew how to get it, and get it fast.

Most grandchildren never get the opportunity to know their great-grandparents. Amy never knew our great-grandfather. That is why this story is so unbelievable.

It was another evening of card games and fun at the cottage. What happened that evening has left an impression on all of us, especially my grandmother. Her father had passed away several years earlier. Some of her many keepsakes after his death included his cap, his pipe, and his canes. He had his cap for several years and smoked his pipe even longer. It seemed it was his trademark.

The card game came to an abrupt halt when Amy walked into the room.

She was wearing the cap, worn to the side as he wore it, she had the pipe dangling from the side of her mouth as he did, and she walked with his canes as she said the words "I'm Poppa."

To this day we will never know how Amy knew he wore that cap and smoked that pipe. She had absolutely no prior knowledge of our great-grandfather, no one had ever told her stories of him, or showed her pictures. How did she know "the man she never knew," was called Poppa?

CHAPTER NINETEEN
PLAY BALL

My parents wanted Amy to play sports with regular kids just as much as they wanted her integrated in regular classrooms. She played well. I'm not sure what made her play better, the fact that she was ambidextrous, or the fact that she watched sports so much on television that she played like a professional. The moment she put on her batting gloves and helmet, she became a player.

Amy's ability to handle certain situations was incredible. My parents had signed Amy up for a league that played once a week in Bridgenorth, a town just north of Peterborough. At that time, Amy had her tracheotomy. I went with her to her first game. When we walked up to the field, the girls had already started their warm-ups. It was announced that a new player had arrived to join the team. As Amy and I walked onto the field, the girls surrounded us. Amy stood in the middle as every girl stared in amazement at her. For the most part children are very innocent when it comes to staring. After all, Amy was different. Not only was she different but she was breathing through something on her neck. This time there were no parents standing close by to say the ever popular words, "It's not polite to stare sweetie."

As I looked around the circle of girls, I could feel my face getting flush. Looking at their facial expressions was unbearable. With every bone in my body I wanted to scream, "Quit staring at her damnit! She's not some freak or alien."

Before a word left my mouth Amy began to talk to the girls. And before I knew it, they were laughing. I was used to people staring at her. Why shouldn't she be used to it, too? It didn't matter to her. She turned an uncomfortable situation into a funny one. I shouldn't have expected any less from her.

Amy became a great addition to that baseball team. Every team she played for was lucky to have her. She was a great player and an entertainer, too. When she stepped up to the plate, she became a player. She could catch, throw, scuff the ground in the batter's box, spit, and switch-hit. Everything a professional does when they step up to the plate, Amy did.

Amy at baseball camp

CHAPTER TWENTY
SPILLS AND THRILLS

I spent most of my childhood dreaming of having a horse of my own. Like most parents, I'm sure mine wanted to be sure this was something I was going to stick with before investing a large sum of money to purchase one and board it. So, I went to horse camp every year, and thoroughly enjoyed every minute of it.

For as much as I enjoyed show day at camp I also did not look forward to it. It symbolized the end of a glorious week of riding twice daily, trail rides, swimming, arts and crafts, mucking stalls, and just plain fun. I rode a different horse every year and found something special in each of them.

My first year I rode a Thoroughbred mix named Sam. She had a Canadian Sport Horse look to her, a beautiful dapple-grey that stood at approximately 16 hands high. My instructor worried that she may be too much horse for me, but of course I insisted that I would be able to manage despite the fact that I needed a leg-up every time I rode her. We got to know each other well throughout the course of the week and we cleaned up on show day. We had a little trouble with the game called Musical Frisbee. A row of Frisbees lined the center of the ring, and just like in Musical Chairs we rode around the Frisbees and when the music stopped we had to dismount and grab a Frisbee. The one without a Frisbee was eliminated. Seeing as how Sam was such a tall horse, it was a long way to the ground to dismount quickly and remount when the music started again, but we managed.

We had a slight problem with the saddlebag race. Lined up at one end of the arena we stood on horseback waiting for our partner to ride to us, pass us the bag, and we were to ride to the end of the ring and place our bag on the fence at the other end. Even the quietest of horses may have problem with a "posse" of horses riding straight for them at full speed. In a cloud of dust my partner finally came into view. Unfortunately, she could not get close enough to pass the saddlebag so she tossed it. Even though I understood the saddlebag was coming, there was absolutely no warning for poor Sam. All of the sudden a large, dark object was hurling toward her. Remarkably I was able to catch the bag, but not before Sam took off like a shot. We were heading for the other end of the arena at full speed. There was no stopping Sam. As far as she was concerned, the unidentified object was hot on her trail and she was not about to stop.

The fence was fast approaching. I had two choices: make her stop or bail out. Since the first choice didn't even seem to be an option as far as Sam was concerned, I chose the latter. I knew that at least one of us would get hurt if I tried to ride through it. And I certainly wasn't prepared to try to jump the fence. After all, this was my first year at camp, and I was riding western. I had made no attempt at jumping yet, especially not a fence that was easily 4 ½ feet tall. Before I bailed out I had one last vision, what if she puts on the brakes just before the fence and sends me in orbit to the *other* side of the fence? At the last possible second I threw myself to the ground. I don't know what it feels like to jump out of a moving vehicle but I think I got a pretty good idea that day. Sitting on the sidelines was my family, including Amy, watching the entire ordeal unfold. I had bailed out of the saddle to the right and Sam went left.

When I stood up, I had tears streaming down my face and by the time my instructor reached me, I was laughing. My emotions were entirely too mixed up for me to do anything but laugh because I was okay.

I made it through one of my first traumatic episodes on horseback and I had to do what I tell my students these days, "If you're not hurt, you better get back up there."

I think I knew if I didn't get back on that day I may never get back on another horse and the thought of that, well, it was unthinkable.

Amy has seen me take some spills off many a horse; it's all part of learning to ride I suppose. That may be why she was a little hesitant when it came to getting on all the horses I have put her on. On average it may have taken her approximately 5 minutes to get on, and it was a long, slow, cautious process. Once aboard she was beaming with delight. When she was happy her favorite word was "wonderful!" She said it with such enthusiasm, we giggled whenever she said it, thus encouraging her to say it whenever she wanted to see us smile. I can't count how many times I've heard it. I still use it, but it has to be said the same way with the same emphasis on the syllables as she used to use.

She put her trust and faith in me and my judgment and enjoyed every horse she rode. A short ride was usually all it was, but it was always enough for her. I am so happy I was able to make horses a part of her life, too. There are many children who never visit a farm, much less ride horses and a take part in feeding and caring for them. Amy thrived on it, especially the feeding aspect. She enjoyed her food and assumed animals did, too.

After four years of camp, my parents finally agreed that this was something that was in my blood. This phrase is very common amongst people in the horse industry. It's so addictive you can't seem to get rid of it. Once it's there, it's there, and there's not a thing you can do about it. So when I was fourteen, I got my first pony, Windy. Until then I had the rest of my family to help care for our pets. Windy was my responsibility. I had very little to work with for equipment seeing as how this was my first experience as a horse owner, but I managed. I had to find every way imaginable to make owning Windy a possibility. This included a bareback pad for a saddle, a used bridle that was slightly too big and most definitely on its last legs (I used electrical tape to hold it together), and a grooming kit that had just the basics.

Windy stayed at my friend Krista's, the one who lived on the farm directly behind us. So I never had far to walk to visit my pony and I could see him across the field from my bedroom window. He was *my* pony, therefore I had the power to choose who could and could not ride him. When Amy wanted to ride, I always found the time. It usually meant leading her around in the backyard or in the field just behind us. What made it even more enjoyable for her was the fact that it wasn't far up to get on him, which meant it wasn't far to fall either. After one safe trip around the yard she would start to loosen up and giggle with every step Windy took. It was always a pleasure to take her for a ride. And it never mattered whether the ride lasted two minutes or ten, she cherished every moment as if it was her first time ever on horseback.

CHAPTER TWENTY-ONE
DON'T CRY

School became one of Amy's greatest loves. There aren't many children in this world who don't like Saturday mornings, holidays, and of course being snowed in. As I said before Amy was different. It wasn't unusual for her to be upset about missing school. She was very involved in every aspect, including sports. Kendra and Amy went to a Catholic school and I went to a public school.

I liked school and loved the extra-curricular activities even more. Aside from playing sports, I enjoyed drama class. My first year of high school I landed the big part of the wizard's cat in *Once Upon a Mattress,* a spin-off of *The Princess and the Pea.* Above all the laughter in the crowd, I could hear Amy's little chuckle. I knew she was focusing on me and me only. To this day I'm not sure whether she understood the antics of the Queen and her servants, or if she just thought her older sister looked pretty darn silly dressed up like a cat and crawling around on all fours. I was the cat who could walk on either four or two legs and stand up and sing along with the rest of the cast.

My second year of high school, a team of ten students was chosen to develop and write a very involved and very emotional script for a play we called *Drao.* Through a series of exercises and small scenes we created a play that said a little about all of us. Quite surprisingly we found that each of our scenes were related to something that had deeply impacted each of our lives.

My scene portrayed a young couple that had recently split up and the boy was treating the young girl with little to no respect.

I exploded into my scene with the line, "Do unto others as you would have them do unto you!"

The young girl is crying because the young man has treated her so badly. The first time I played the part in front of the entire school I worried so much about the crying in my scene that I cried so hard I forgot my lines. Thank goodness for the prompter.

When Amy came to the evening showing of the play, I wondered how much she'd understand. I belted out my opening line and the crowd was silent. It was my first play where I had everyone's undivided attention. As the scene went on, and I began to cry I got very deep into my part as many actors do.

It was going great, a command performance, but the silence was broken when a small voice shouted out from the crowd, "Don't cry Deanne!"

Somebody else had stolen the stage. When I held my face in my hands supposedly crying, I fought back the laughter and smiled. That's my sister.

CHAPTER TWENTY-TWO
MY MOLSON

For many years Molson was the dog we adored, the dog we played with, the dog we swam with, went fishing with, went everywhere with. The happiness came to an abrupt halt the day I came home to an empty house and got a call from Tracey Manning. A yellow lab had been hit, and she thought it was Molson. I ran through the house frantically calling for our dear friend. Much to my dismay, the house was silent. I called our neighbor, and asked him to take me to the dog. Wrapped in a burlap bag on the side of the road was our dear Molson. I went home to call my father; he was in town at my aunt and uncle's. When he came to the phone I couldn't get the words out. I choked back my tears; all I could say was "Molson."

How were we going to tell Amy? The only death she had semi-understood was the passing of our cousins' dog, Goliath. The Woodsides had Goliath, a Maltese, for several years. Amy loved him, too, but due to health problems he had to be put to sleep. We had all spoke of Heaven, and did our best to explain to Amy that Molson was with Goliath now.

It was winter and the ground was frozen. The only possible burial ground for Molson was at the dealership where my father worked. There was a tractor there that could dig a hole through the frozen ground. A wooden cross marked his grave. For years Amy spoke of Molson. She cried for him daily, for weeks, even months. My parents were beginning to wonder if she'd ever get over the loss of her faithful companion. In our eyes he was *her* faithful companion in the truest sense.

I can still see her crying, looking through the window in the door, and saying, "I miss my Molson."

Molson's private cemetery was on Highway 7 on the road to our grandparents, on the road to the cottage, on the road to my work. You can imagine how often we passed his gravesite. Not once did we pass it without Amy mentioning his name. It became a habit, even if she wasn't in the car – we thought of him. He will *never* be forgotten.

CHAPTER TWENTY-THREE
THE PIÑATA

Christmas was always a time for family. It usually involved a gathering at one of the five families' homes. Both of my parents had four siblings in their families.

One Christmas we went to a hotel in Midland near the Palmer family. This was a neat change for all of us. Instead of worrying about all the hassles of cooking and cleaning up, not to mention where everyone was going to sleep, we let the hotel take care of everything. Besides, the kids all liked to swim, especially Amy, and the hotel had an indoor swimming pool.

Another year we decided it would be fun to take a trip to Florida. A van was rented and we piled as many as possible into the van, and another car, and set off for Florida, destination, Disney World. What a road trip that was. When we arrived, the weather was horrible. We were the Crazy Canadians determined to experience it all, including the water park. Many of the local people were wearing sweaters and long pants, some even wore hats and gloves. And there we were, in bathing suits, riding the few water rides that were open. Nothing would deter us from enjoying everything they had to offer.

After a glorious stay at the resort, we loaded back up for the trip north. Along the way we stopped at a hotel for a much needed rest and break from the tight quarters in the van. Aunt Lynn and Uncle Pete, most often referred to as "Uncle Peach" by Amy, had brought a piñata for the kids. And we all know how kids are when it comes to piñatas. It very quickly became the highlight of the evening. We all lined up to take our shot at busting open the paper-maché figure full of candy. Blindfold or no blindfold this was pure entertainment for all, young and old.

Amy waited patiently for her turn to take a whack at it. She giggled, and rolled around in a ball of laughter, almost taunting her cousins and sisters as we all took our turn. Then, it was Amy's turn.

She took her weapon and stepped up to the piñata swinging with all her might. After a few swings and misses and then a bump that merely moved it to the side leaving it swinging back and forth, the piñata now seemed to be taunting her. All of the sudden this wasn't so funny anymore. Amy's expression had drastically changed. This was no longer a game; it was time to get serious.

Before taking yet another blow, she belted out the words, "Hold still, you son of a bitch!"

That statement from *innocent little nine-year-old Amy* turned the entire room into a huge ball of laughter.

CHAPTER TWENTY-FOUR
DON'T BE SUCH A BABY

Despite the fact that Amy was constantly battling her weight, you couldn't slow her down. She enjoyed all sports especially riding her bike. Like everyone else, even the best, most experienced rider will take a spill, or wipe out. One day she took her bike out for what turned out to be a very short ride. She didn't get far, just to the corner before she took her spill. It wasn't the first and most definitely wouldn't be the last. With tears in her eyes, and a few scrapes she hobbled home; she was only four houses away. Mom doctored her wounds and helped her up to her room. She had a room like any other teenage kid, filled with posters of animals, and her favorite singer, Michael Jackson, a television, a VCR, movies, and video games. It was more than enough to keep her occupied while her wounds healed.

Amy stayed in her room for the rest of the evening. This was not uncommon for her. She loved her room; it had everything she needed to entertain her for hours on end. Her video collection could outnumber the local video store, and she knew every line to every one of them.

The next morning when she got up she hopped on one foot to the restroom. She kept complaining about her leg. It was not unusual for Amy to play things up when she was hurt, or just plain wanted some extra attention. We could have rewritten the old story "Never Cry Wolf" several different ways to fit Amy and her antics.

I can still hear her telling Mom, "My leg, my leg."

Assuming that this was another one of her pranks my mother said, "Oh Amy, don't be such a baby."

No one had witnessed her fall. But Amy was carrying this "prank" on just a little too long. Mom decided she had better take Amy to the doctor's office. You can imagine how horrible she felt when the x-ray results confirmed a fracture. There was no "crying wolf" any longer. I think Amy knew how much we regretted our lack of attention toward her and how we wanted to take back all of our comments. Before her cast came off she once again was in the spotlight. She soaked in every second of attention we had to offer, and there wasn't a square inch left on that cast to sign.

CHAPTER TWENTY-FIVE
YOU NEVER BITE THE HAND THAT FEEDS YOU

Throughout my high school years I was able to participate in the Co-op Program. I had the wonderful opportunity to work on a horse farm. I say wonderful only because it really was wonderful to work with horses and earn school credits for it. The program is designed to help students gain work experience and to possibly get a job placement in the student's area of interest. My area of interest has always been with horses. Working at Neitek Farms for John Neill was a unique and rewarding job. It helped to give me a solid background in the knowledge of horses, and the experience I gained help make me the horseperson I am today.

My job included mucking stalls, which comes with any horse job, exercising the racehorses, assisting the veterinarian, helping with breeding, and working with the mares and foals. I couldn't have found a better way to spend my afternoons then to go to the farm. My mother picked me up from school and drove me out there daily. After working there for several weeks, and my friends and family hearing me talk non-stop about "what happened at the barn today," I asked my mother to stay and watch me work one day. I was proud to show and tell everyone where I worked, including my sister.

Everyone knew about Amy's fascination with animals. Watching her around new animals was both scary and amazing. To see a child walk up to a strange dog is scary. But to watch a small child approach over 1,000 pounds of horse is another fear all together. Of all the horses Amy should choose to approach first– it would have to be the biggest and strongest in the barn – the stallion.

Cash 'N Balance was a stallion admired by many; a chestnut Quarter Horse with a bold white blaze – which most of his offspring inherited. Like many of us he had good days and bad days. Cleaning his stall was sometimes an adventure. One day he'd be so ornery he'd have to be tied and I'd work around him. Other days he would be so kind as to lower his head to my chest and let me scratch his big chestnut jowls and his big white forehead, I learned to respect his space, some days you just don't want to be messed with.

Much like she did with people – Amy captured Cash's heart, too. She came into the barn, picked up a handful of hay and walked right up to his stall. He came to the window in his stall and lowered his head to meet hers. Gently his lips flapped together softly to take in every blade she had to offer. She giggled with delight. Every time she came to the barn from that day forward, Cash knew her. It didn't matter what kind of day he was having. When Amy approached his stall, his demeanor changed from a stallion to that of an old gelding that couldn't be calmer; he was almost stoic. Needless to say, John and I were absolutely amazed with the relationship that had developed between Amy and Cash.

CHAPTER TWENTY-SIX
THE PUPPY

Quarter Horses and Thoroughbreds weren't the only things that kept me coming back to work for John year after year. Over the years we had become friends, too. I took Amy there on several occasions and she thoroughly enjoyed her visits to the farm. She always wanted to feed the horses, play with the dogs, and give John one of her famous hugs.

As soon as he saw her he'd ask, "Hey Amy, where's my hug?"

She never seemed to run short on those hugs of hers. She knew she'd get a treat from him almost every time she visited, and it almost seemed as though she could do no wrong through John's eyes.

Aside from breeding horses, John bred dogs as well. You can image how thrilled Amy was every time I took her to John's. Not only did she see her old buddies John and Cash, but if there wasn't a foal to see you could usually find a litter of puppies. The puppies and their mom always had their own room.

On this particular occasion, their room was the laundry room. There was a large cage for the mom and her babies and a tile floor for them to crawl around on when they were old enough to explore. It made a quiet, cozy little den for the females to have their litters undisturbed from the others.

Like most children, Amy was enthralled with puppies. It was quite evident she loved all animals, especially baby ones. I took her to the laundry room/den for quick visit with the puppies. She knew to be gentle. She was very conscious of how she handled each of them and moved slowly around "Mommy and her babies." While Amy was spending her glorious moments with the puppies I did my routine check on each pup and their mother. I cleaned and refilled their water bowl and checked their bedding. When I finished, I convinced Amy it was time to let the puppies sleep, so they could grow up to be big and strong. She was hesitant but she understood and agreed to leave the puppies until the next time we could visit.

The moment I got in the door at home, my parents told me that John had called. He had told them that the litter of pups was one pup short. I couldn't understand it. The head count I had taken just minutes ago had matched. I explained everything to my parents, being sure to include every little detail. I wasn't far into my explanation when my parents turned to Amy.

Recalling a similar incident, my dad picked up the phone and called John. Several years earlier, Amy had put one of our pet rabbits in the dryer. He asked John to look in the dryer. John found the missing puppy, unharmed, but in the dryer. When the phone call ended, Amy knew she was in trouble. She knew exactly what was going on and who was about to be sent to her room. It certainly wasn't me.

To this day, I don't know what Amy was thinking. Perhaps she thought she could sneak it home if I didn't see it, or come back for it later. Nevertheless, she had hidden that puppy; there was no other possible explanation. The next time we went to John's, Amy apologized, and of course she was forgiven.

CHAPTER TWENTY-SEVEN
A LITTLE DIRT NEVER HURT ANYBODY

I always knew I wanted to pursue a career with horses. I also knew I enjoyed working with people. I couldn't think of a better program to take in college than the Equestrian Coaching Program. It would combine the two together – I could work with both horses and people of all ages.

In the fall of '89 I attended Humber College in Etobicoke, Ontario, just north of Toronto. As much as I didn't want to leave home, I was thrilled to be embarking on such an exciting adventure. I couldn't think of a better way to earn a college degree.

Moving away from home for the first time was a big step, as it is for many. I hated saying goodbye to my family, especially Amy. She seemed to understand it wasn't forever. I thought Kendra and her would be fighting over my room, as many younger siblings do, but that didn't happen. It was still my room and Amy just spent a lot of time in it. My room was the best in the house, or so I thought. The entire attic was my teen pad. My bedroom was three quarters of the attic and the back quarter was my sitting room. That room had my stuffed animal collection, my stereo, and some big pillows, and I covered every inch of wall space with posters. The only drawback to living in the attic was the occasional hot summer night. My room was like a sauna.

I moved into the college dorm, which unfortunately was not on campus. What a change from an entire attic to a small room with a small bed, a little bit of closet space, and a small sink. My sitting room was bigger than my dorm room. What made matters even worse was the fact that the Toronto Transit Commission was on strike. We had to walk to the bus stop and wait for a bus. On the very rare occasion that a bus would actually drive by, it would be so full we had to fight to get on and squish in together or the bus wouldn't even stop to take on more passengers. This wouldn't have been such a problem if it hadn't been for the fact that we had to be at school, in the barn at 7 am. If we were late – it affected our grades.

Shortly after school started, we had an in-house schooling show. I had been riding racehorses for the past couple of years and therefore had not received much in the way of formal instruction. It is, needless to say, a different style of riding all together. I decided it would be best to enter the jumper classes as opposed to the hunter classes. My riding style would not be judged in a jumper class like it would in a hunter class. A clear round with no faults would probably get me in the ribbons. The only thing I needed was a reliable Schoolie; this term is used at many facilities for their horses used for riding lessons. I was lucky enough to get one of the best Schoolies in the barn named Jaspis. Despite the fact that he was missing half of his tongue, he was an honest gelding that just needed to be pointed in the right direction.

A couple of us had decided we would be brave and enter the open jumper class. Looking back, I would take away the word *brave* and enter *stupid* in its place. The open class was the last class of the day and usually the most exciting. Little did we know, we were about to be the *entertainment* of the day. A second year student had designed the course. The smallest fence was four feet high. For someone who had not jumped a course of fences since she was fourteen at horse camp, these jumps seemed Olympic size.

Despite the size of the jumps, the difficulty of the course and my lack of experience, I still said, "What the hell."

I look back now and say, "What the hell was I thinking!"

The bleachers were filled with family members and fellow students. And right in the middle on the top row sat my parents and my sisters. Amy had spent most of her day walking up and down all the aisles, making sure to meet and feed every horse she could before taking her seat in the bleachers with everyone else. When my number was called I entered the ring with a combination of butterflies and queasiness in my stomach. I had watched the competitors before me knock down fences, go off course, and even fall off their horses. So, I took a deep breath and entered the ring.

"What the hell right?"

Jaspis was a pro. If it weren't for his willingness to jump whatever was in front of him, I never would have made it through the course. With every fence we took I felt I was jumping seven feet instead of four. As Jaspis cleared fences my chest met the crest of his neck, I saw nothing but mane. I clenched my lower leg against his side to help keep my balance after the third fence, which was a mistake. I lost my stirrups. Frantically searching for them, Jaspis felt my legs moving and thought I was asking him to move on. Our pace quickened. I continued through the course without my stirrups, hanging on for dear life, and Jaspis never missed a beat.

The end of the course finished with a combination followed by a sharp turn to the left to the final fence. Upon completing the second fence in the combination, there was enough room to squeeze in three strides, if we were lucky, and the sharp turn was to be included in those three short strides. Going straight and missing the last fence wasn't even an option.

After landing from the combination we were less than two strides away from the warm-up ring. It had been roped off as a holding area or small area to walk and keep you and your horse warm while waiting your turn in the ring. And since this was such entertainment for everyone, there was a line-up of competitors on horseback watching this all unfold.

We finished the combination with me barely hanging on, and without thinking Jaspis made his turn for the final fence. I, on the other hand, headed straight for the warm-up ring. We've all seen the cartoon where the horse turns on a dime and the rider goes straight without his/her horse under him. That was me, and without a horse under me, gravity took over. When I landed, I rolled over on my side. As I sat up I spit the dirt from my mouth.

The audience was silent until a familiar voice yelled, "Oh my God, Deanne!"

Without looking I replied, "I'm okay, Amy."

I looked over at Jaspis. He stood only a few feet away, and was probably just as stunned as I was. I gathered the reins and got back on. We only had one fence left, nothing was broken and we had no faults.

We had to finish. We cleared the last fence and therefore had a clear round. Only one other rider went clear. Iaspis and I took the second place ribbon, despite the fact that I fell off before the last fence.

CHAPTER TWENTY-EIGHT
JAMMER

In the fall of '89 I worked part time for John Neill. I was one of the lucky students in the Co-op program to be offered a job upon completion of my course. I had given up my pony while in high school and leased a Quarter Horse for a summer. But I longed for a horse of my own again. In a small group of weanlings I worked with I became quite attached to a filly and colt. The filly was a cuddler. She was later named Kisses and Cuddles. It seemed appropriate. She loved attention, almost craved it. When I went to their field to feed them, she was always first in line to the feed bucket and then first in line for attention shortly thereafter. I had exercised her mother Peanut and she had been one of my favorite mares at the farm. I guess her sweet demeanor had been passed on. Like many other mares she could be a little moody as some might say. When things didn't go her way, she let you know it. But I loved her anyway.

The colt was the exact opposite of the filly. He wasn't mean in any way, just a little shy maybe. He stayed by his mother's side and when I got close enough to pet him he enjoyed it for only a moment before heading in the other direction. He was a challenge. So I took it upon myself to spend time with him whenever possible to help him realize that my hands were gentle and could be trusted.

John always knew I wanted another horse and whenever I spoke of the filly, he always asked, "What do you think of that little colt?"

Before I knew it I was filling out registration papers for my very own *Appendix Quarter Horse*, and choosing a name for the shy little fellow. He came to be known as Jammer, named after a horse in his bloodlines, Jammed Lucky. He grew to be a 16 hands high, beautiful bay horse that I have enjoyed for many years, and hopefully many to come. Through the help and advice of others, I trained him to the best of my ability. This was my first true test in training a young horse.

As many trainers will say, we had our good days and our bad days.

Inevitably in every horse's career there are days you do not feel like working, much like people. I can recall days when before mounting, Jammer would do a little dance around me. His antics didn't stop me from riding him, but more than I care to remember he wasn't tip-toeing around my feet either. On occasion I rode with one or more throbbing toes. But I believe Jammer and I have definitely come to an agreement and the hours, weeks and years I have spent with him have helped make him the horse he is today.

Amy riding behind the scenes at a rodeo

What amazed me was the way he behaved when Amy was around. As much as I would like to take credit for his good behavior in her presence, I think he, like so many other animals, knew there was something different about Amy. She was special and he made exceptions on her behalf, despite the day he was having or the mood he was in. It didn't bother him that it took her longer than most to get on. She spoke to him the entire time. I taught her phrases like, "It's okay Jammer," "Easy Jammer," and "Jammer whoa," not that she ever needed that one. Looking back, I think it may have eased *her* mind more than his.

Once she made it in the saddle it wasn't long before she took the reins and she was in control. Amy became an equestrian, just as she became a ball player when she stepped up to the plate. She had been watching me ride for so many years. She knew how to turn left and right, how to ask him to back up and of course how to stop. As long as I was close by, she was confident. I could walk a few paces in front of Jammer and he would follow my every move with his head held low. Occasionally, she would ask for a trot. I would jog ahead and tell her to give Jammer the cue and he always had a smooth transition into a slow western jog. His feet barely left the ground, giving Amy a smooth ride, at just little faster pace. She loved every moment and I have to admit so did I.

CHAPTER TWENTY-NINE
AMY RIDES THE TRAILS

After completing the coaching program at Humber, I had the opportunity to work at Claireville Ranch. It is located on a conservation area not far from Brampton, Ontario, just north of Toronto. Throughout the summer a day camp is available for kids, trail rides are available daily, every hour, seven days a week and hay rides for large groups. Through the winter months the ranch is open on the weekends for trail rides and sleigh rides, weather permitting. I took on both the management and instructor's positions.

The scenery and trails are beautiful, as one can imagine, seeing as how the ranch is located on a conservation area. This also means the wildlife is plentiful. It was not uncommon to see several deer while riding through the trails.

In conversation with many of our customers we often heard, "You must love your job."

It is incredible how peaceful and beautiful it could be in an area so close to Toronto. The trails took us alongside and through rivers or small streams, deep into the woods, up an embankment that overlooked pastures for the horses, and to the tops of hills that looked down on fields that were untouched. It is a little piece of Heaven, not far from the headaches of a big city.

Just as with my many other jobs in the horse industry, I was proud of my work and loved to bring friends and family to see my "fun" that was supposedly "work." I wanted everyone to experience the beauty of the conservation area on horseback. When my parents came to visit, I asked them if they would like to go for a ride. I chose the quietest of the bunch for my mom and Amy and we headed for the trails. Before long we were down in the valley and to a spot where I felt we could go for a short jog. I asked my lead horse to pick up the pace. As my horse jogged along I turned around in the saddle to see how everyone was doing. My mother was on the horse behind me and she was laughing hysterically. When I looked past my mother and saw Amy's face I brought my horse back down to a walk. Her face was red and she was not having fun. For some horses, the trot is not the smoothest gait to ride. Apparently I had chosen a rather bumpy ride for Amy.

My mother could hear Amy's pleas from behind and could not stop laughing. Once the horses were all back to a walk, she continued to laugh and Amy sighed a breath of relief. I rode back alongside Amy and her mount and asked her what was wrong.

When she finally caught her breath she replied; "I hurt my pants."

She had been telling my mother between bounces, "My pants, it's hurting my pants. I don't want to 'joggle' anymore."

I couldn't help but laugh with my mother. For most, it is the buttocks that hurt when trying to sit to the trot of a bouncy horse, but for Amy it was her pants. She soon realized that what she had said was humorous and she joined in our laughter even though it was at her discomfort.

CHAPTER THIRTY
UNSPORTSMANLIKE CONDUCT

Amy was a true competitor in every sport she could participate in. She was a great spectator as well. I sometimes thought she enjoyed sitting on the sidelines as much as she enjoyed competing. There were games she attended where she cheered for both teams. Even though that might have been somewhat confusing to others, when I look back now, I think she simply enjoyed seeing others celebrate, and she loved to join in the fun.

As many have said, "It doesn't matter whether you win or lose, just have some fun."

She was a team player in the truest form. Her words of encouragement could be heard over the biggest of crowds. And when it came to individual sports, she was just as supportive. She was always one of the first to congratulate a fellow competitor or give them a pat on the back. Over the years, she attended several Special Olympic competitions, and she was a winner in every sport. I couldn't count the number of trophies or medals she has won. There is a shelf at my parents' house that holds the many photos, medals and memories from the events she participated in. Whether it was speed skating, swimming, or track and field, she always gave 110 percent in every event.

Despite the fact that Amy had a "disability," there were times she showed us she could be just like the rest of us. She loved to impress her friends and family and as she grew older there were times she wanted to impress certain people who she took a particular *liking* to. It was quite evident to all of us that Amy had the same feelings many teenagers get once puberty hits. When she wanted to "impress" certain boys or men, she found a way to get her message out loud and clear. She teased, flirted, and blushed just like any young girl in love. If things weren't going her way, she got her point across, and usually loud enough to make everyone stop and look.

Amy under the basketball hoop on Chamberlain Street

Much of Amy's social life existed through Special Olympics. On one particular occasion, she grew fond of one of her coaches. At a cross-country skiing event, Amy wanted more than ever to "bring home the gold," and impress her coach. Throughout the entire race Amy held a solid position guaranteeing her a medal. As always she was giving it her "all" even then some with the hopes of getting a congratulatory hug from her coach. Her glorious vision was shattered when she lost her balance and fell.

In the process of getting back on her feet another competitor passed her. Amy was furious. In that moment we saw just how "normal" Amy could be. Many of us have been in this position, but not all of us have had the guts to do what Amy did next.

Without a moment's hesitation, Amy belted out the words, "Get back here you bitch!"

It was at that particular time many of us realized that winning could be just as important to someone like Amy as it is to everyone else. Not only did she show us her competitiveness, but also she showed us we should persevere and never give up. Her strength and courage shone that day. She got back on her feet and continued on.

In the end, she won in more ways than one. She got her gold medal, her spot on the podium, but most of all, the smile and the hug she envisioned from the very beginning.

CHAPTER THIRTY-ONE
GRANDPARENTS

Like many young children, we loved to visit our grandparents. We spent many a weekend at Grandma Helen's place. Our Saturdays included learning to sew, write calligraphy, and drink tea like "little ladies." And if we were lucky, she'd read us our "fortune" in the tea leaves when we were through. The evening usually involved a night by the organ learning songs of yesterday or practicing our Christmas carols for the senior's home we performed at.

Amy thoroughly enjoyed this. Not only did she get to be "in the spotlight" but also she seemed to take a special interest in socializing with the residents. For some reason she was very drawn to them, and you could tell they enjoyed it just as much as she did.

On Sunday mornings Grandma and "her three girls" went to church. Amy and Kendra attended a Catholic school, and through Sunday school and religion classes at her daily school, Amy became a true believer in God and Heaven. It was incredible how much she understood. You never realized how much she was paying attention until she surprised you with her amazing capability to comfort both you and herself in a sad, sometimes tragic situation.

As much as we enjoyed visiting Grandma Helen, we loved visiting Grandma and Granddad Cassidy. They lived on a farm in Tweed, Ontario. I don't know a child to this day who doesn't like to go to a farm. Some of my fondest memories from the farm include: feeding the ducks, going to the river to fish or swim, doing crafts, playing cards, helping Grandma cook or bake, and watching Granddad work in the shop on the many trinkets and machines he had collected over the years. We loved exploring through the barn that had been retired many years ago even though we weren't really supposed to be in there. My grandfather was a great collector. He had tools, machines, and supplies that were considered to be antiques even artifacts to many people. And like any adult, he didn't want us

Standing left to right, Grandma Nora Cassidy, Granddad Ray Cassidy,Grandma Helen Tucker

to get hurt so some parts of the barn were "off limits."

The best times were had tobogganing, snowmobiling, and cutting the grass. This was a big treat because Granddad had a riding lawnmower. We used to fight over who cut the grass first. And at the end of the day we fought over who got to sit on Grandma's lap first in the rocking chair by the wood stove. It was the perfect ending to a perfect day.

Amy and Granddad shared a special bond. She adored both of our grandmothers but what she had with Granddad was unique. They teased each other until they were laughing hysterically, and sometimes it didn't stop there. It was wonderful watching the two of them together. He was always the first one up in the morning; I could hear his footsteps from my bed. And Amy couldn't wait for another day to begin with Granddad. It always meant another day of teasing, laughter, treats, and most importantly, all the attention she could handle in one day. We all enjoyed every moment we spent with Granddad.

In the summer of 1993, Granddad's health began to deteriorate. He suffered from a series of strokes. It was a difficult time for all of us, including Granddad. His memory was affected greatly just before Christmas. He asked my grandmother to sit down with him and go through their photo albums to refresh his memory on all the faces that were no longer familiar to him. Despite his illness, he was determined to make this as easy as possible for his family. That's just the kind of person he was. I admired him greatly.

The following year he was in and out of the hospital. He refused to stay in the hospital like many elderly people do. It was evident to all of us that his day to leave us was drawing near, and he wished to be at home with my grandmother and nowhere else. In October of 1994, he passed away at the farm in my grandmother's arms.

Explaining the death of a loved one to a child has got to be one of the most difficult tasks. We had a hard time helping Amy say goodbye to her beloved friend Molson. Now we had to tell her Granddad was no longer with us but in Heaven. I remember telling her Granddad had gone to be with Molson. It seemed to be the best way to explain it to her. It was one of the most difficult times my family had experienced and we came together to grieve over the loss of such a great man.

After the funeral we all sat in the kitchen at the farm, reminiscing of days gone by and shedding what few tears we had left for the day. Amy went to my grandmother's side. She couldn't stand to see any of us crying. Grandma was sitting at the table in Granddad's chair with tears in her eyes.

Amy put her hand on Grandma's back and said, "Don't worry Grandma, Granddad's with Him now." She pointed to the crucifix hanging on the wall. Those words brought comfort to each and every one of us in that room. It was comfort knowing Granddad was in Heaven, and comfort knowing that Amy understood. Maybe more than we'll ever know.

CHAPTER THIRTY-TWO

SOMEBODY SPECIAL IS WATCHING OVER YOU

The summer before my grandfather became ill, I met my husband Jimmy. He was in the U.S. Army, stationed at Fort Drum in New York. We spent a great deal of time together, and it wasn't long before I was taking him home to Peterborough to meet my family.

I always knew my parents and family would welcome anyone I brought home. They were very outgoing and they made everyone feel at home. My favorite part about bringing a new friend home was watching them meet Amy for the first time. I always knew their reactions to her said a lot about their character. She put them to the test with her antics and pranks.

The first time Jimmy met her she was in the backyard playing basketball.

Before he had the chance to say "Hello Amy, nice to meet you" she threw the ball to him and asked him to play. The two of them played basketball for over an hour. Later, Jimmy told me how he had never really had the opportunity to meet a child with Down Syndrome and she made it so easy. The two of them got along great. She welcomed him with open arms every time from that day on.

It always made me happy to hear her ask, "Where's Jimmy?"

Before long, we were engaged, and Amy was thrilled. She covered her mouth and giggled every time we told her he was going to be my husband.

The following January we got married in Watertown, New York. We decided to have a small ceremony in January with a large wedding in June. Despite the fact that the first wedding was small and at a courthouse in downtown Watertown at 8:30 in the morning, my family made it a special one. My parents and sisters came, both of my grandmothers were there, and my Aunt June and Uncle Jim stood up for us as matron of honor and best man. All of them came bearing gifts. We had homemade cake, keepsakes were passed down, and my aunt made a corsage and bouquet for Jimmy and me. They brought everything to help make it a small but special day for all of us. And what's a wedding day without a few tears being shed?

After the ceremony, Amy came up to me with tears in her eyes she gave me a big hug and said, "I'm so proud of you, Deanne. I love you and Jimmy."

She was the "cake topper" of the day!

We barely got through our wedding in January before plans were underway for the big wedding in June. Before we knew it, the day was upon us. Everything took place at a resort on Rice Lake, just east of Peterborough. It was a beautiful day, a little warmer then Peterborough is used to for a day in the middle of June, but the breeze coming off the lake helped.

We had our pictures taken first, on the dock by the lake. The dinner was next, followed by the ceremony and then the party. It wasn't in the traditional "order" of most weddings, but it was so easy to not have to worry about "getting to the church on time." And thanks to all the help from family and friends, the place looked wonderful, right down to the centerpieces and candy holders (horseshoes and tiny cowboy hats). My Aunt June was able to find the miniature felt hats for the candy and made the centerpieces out of horseshoes with flowers to hold down the balloons. She thought they suited our lifestyles with Jimmy being from Texas and me loving everything to do with horses. They reflected our personalities to a "T."

Amy was so excited. It could have been her wedding day. She loved getting her picture taken and believe me, she was in several of them. She floated around and mingled with everyone, making sure they all knew who was getting married, and where they needed to go. As usual, it was fun to watch her. She took the liberty to walk Grandma Cassidy into the resort.

As they walked up the steps she held Grandma's arm and said, "You know, Grandma, Granddad's watching us."

You can imagine my grandmother's reaction to this statement. There were many occasions we thought Amy might have a "special

Amy congratulating me at the courthouse in
Watertown

connection" with those who are in Heaven. There were too many incidents where she knew facts that had never been revealed to her, and she was so convincing, it was easy to believe her.

CHAPTER THIRTY-THREE
CLIFFORD

Shortly after Jimmy and I got married, he got out of the army and we moved to a farm in Kingston. We spent 24 hours a day, seven days a week together, not to mention the fact that when we first moved there we only had a single bed with no frame. It was a tight fit, but as "newlyweds" we didn't seem to mind.

Many people may say, "It is not a good idea for a married couple to live and work together. You need your space."

Despite the odd quarrel, we look back now and realize it was one of the happiest years of our marriage so far. We lived in a little limestone house with a large farm kitchen, which had a fireplace to keep us "cozy," especially on those cold Canadian nights. We had our cat, our dogs, our horses, and each other and that was all we needed.

We miss the daily chores, the simple lifestyle, my students, and clients and last but not least, the horses. Anyone involved with horses knows there's something about walking into a barn first thing in the morning to hear a friendly whinny from every stall greet you for the day ahead. Jimmy did the maintenance and upkeep, which included snowplowing the driveway. Oddly enough, he enjoyed this job even during the worst of snowstorms. If you asked him today if he misses it, he'd say yes.

Throughout the day I taught lessons, worked with the horses, and mucked stalls. I did some of my best thinking mucking stalls and found the end of the day was just as comforting. The last feed of the day always left me feeling good knowing all my horses were fed and watered and munching happily on their hay for the night.

While living at the farm we acquired a weanling that had a rough start on life. The vet had determined that the colt's mother didn't have enough colostrum in her milk and he was weak and very susceptible to just about anything. It turns out he had developed pneumonia, he was anemic, and to make matters worse, he had stomach ulcers. He was a sad little guy that needed lots of TLC. So we took him in and he was Jimmy's little "project," a project he decided to name Clifford.

The colt had come from a farm that was owned by one of my students. She used the same vet we did. This worked out well as he was familiar with Clifford's history. We spent months trying to nurture the poor little guy, but seemed to be putting more medications into him than anything. It seemed it was going to be a never-ending battle to get Cliff on the road to recovery. Just as we seemed to have one problem cleared up another one came along. Needless to say, he was a small pitiful looking colt that had little to no energy. I can still see Jimmy in Cliff's stall grooming him and Cliff would rest his chin on Jimmy's shoulder the entire time.

At one point I thought, *God he must hate me, every time I come into his stall I'm either shoving medicine down his throat or poking him with a needle.*

The next time Amy came to the farm we wanted to introduce her to our newest family member. We walked to the paddock with her asking every question she could think of, including "why?"

Jammer and Cliff met us at the gate. As we walked through Amy held out her hand for Cliff. Jammer was old news now. The little guy brought his muzzle closer and looked her in the eye. In less than a second, he spun around and kicked up his heels in a playful manner. In the process, his heel caught Amy right in the chest. She didn't feel anything through her thick winter coat. He barely touched her, but it certainly startled her. It was the most action we had seen from him since the day he uneasily stepped off the trailer, or should I say, stumbled. I'm not sure what set him off, but something in the way she smelled or looked sparked a little fire inside the colt that had been sick for several weeks.

Amy never forgot Clifford.

Every time we mentioned his name she would look at us and say, "He kicked me, right here," and she'd point to her chest.

We'd always tell her, "He was just playing Amy."
She knew it, and she'd laugh. I think she knew it all along and just liked to tease us.

CHAPTER THIRTY-FOUR
HIRED HELP

In the summer of '96 we moved to John Neill's place to manage the riding school. We hated to leave all of our clients and friends in Kingston, but we were excited to be moving closer to our family. Instead of being two hours away from them, we were only going to be fifteen minutes away. Needless to say, we were excited, and so was Amy. She clearly understood that we were going to be living at John's place.

Throughout our marriage, almost every time we moved, it rained. The move from Kingston to Peterborough was one of them. You would think that after all the times that I have moved I would be a good packer, but I'm not. I hate packing. The only part I like about moving is the unpacking. I love redecorating and getting settled in, provided there are no broken items.

Believe it or not, moving the horses was probably the easiest part of our move. A lot of our clothes and last minute items got thrown into garbage bags and then into the back of our truck. The moment we were ready to pull out, the rain started. The tarp was on but we knew things were going to be drenched by the time we pulled into John's place.

As with any new home, and in this case a new business as well, there are changes to be made. We started on the inside, clearing all the stalls, washing down the walls, and moving all our tack, equipment and horses in. Then came the outside, the lawn maintenance, flowers and fences. We had decided to paint the fences white, thinking it would match the trim on the barn and give the barn a fresh, clean new look. And so, the chore began.

Amy had been out to visit, stay over and hang out whenever possible. The work never stopped. She would pitch in wherever possible. In the midst of painting the fence and occasionally us, I handed a paintbrush to Amy. She accepted it graciously happy to be a part of "the team."

After an hour or two of painting, chitchat and a few giggles from Amy's humorous antics, she asked a logical question, "Are you going to pay me Dee?"

Thinking it was only fair that she should be paid for her work I answered, "Okay, how much do you want?"

She paused for a moment, maybe a little surprised that I agreed for now she had to decide what her work and time were worth.

Then, very nonchalantly, but quite confidently she said, "Oh, five bucks!"

Regardless of how many hours she may have put in, five dollars seemed reasonable to her. Although it seemed to be enough for Amy, I felt guilty paying her only five dollars for her work, so her pay included a ride on Jammer.

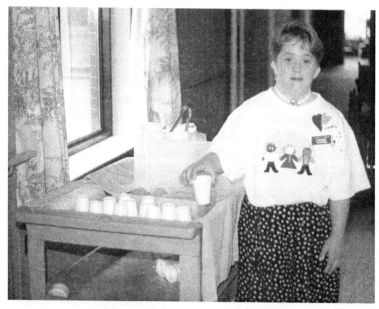

Amy at one of her many volunteer jobs.

CHAPTER THIRTY-FIVE
NEVER SHORT ON HUGS

Amy's hugs were the best. I can't put it any simpler than that. She had one for you whether you needed it or not. I think anyone would agree there were times when you really needed one, and Amy seemed to know it. Other times she might just be plain silly about them. Occasionally she hugged me so hard I couldn't breathe, and then she proceeded to lift me off the ground. Her strength was only surpassed by the love she had to give. And she wasn't stingy with that either.

Just as Amy missed her Molson, and talked about him daily, she missed her grandfather.

She asked so many questions, but seemed to know the answer.

"Granddad is in Heaven."

She knew where the funeral took place and knew exactly where his grave and headstone were in the cemetery. As with all the times she mentioned Molson as we passed his gravesite, she did the same for Granddad. Every time we went to Tweed she asked about Granddad.

My parents took her to visit Granddad's grave. Much like anyone who mourns the death of a loved one, she spoke to him, told him how much she loved him and missed him. But what she did next left an impression and image my family will never forget. After she said all she wanted to say, she laid down on the ground in front of the headstone. She was face down and she spread her arms out to the side.

At first glance she looked like she was making the shape of the cross, but when my mother asked her what she was doing, this was her reply.

"I'm giving Granddad a hug."

Even though our grandfather was not there "in body" to receive one of her heartfelt hugs, I'd like to believe he felt that one, heart and soul. It was genuine and sincere – all of Amy's hugs were. That hug was an extra special one though. She missed her granddad and she "wished" that one all the way to Heaven.

CHAPTER THIRTY-SIX
"YOU *CAN* TEACH AN OLD DOG NEW TRICKS!"

With mixed emotions, Jimmy and I decided to move to Texas, for more reasons than one. We were sad to be leaving my family, but excited about the opportunities for Jimmy. It was time to use his G.I. Bill that he had earned from the Army to attend college. And by attending school in Texas, he would get the most out of this benefit, especially since he was a veteran.

My friend Becky agreed to take care of our horses. John said he would keep our cat Dickens. My cousin Jennifer graciously took Lotus, our loveable Great Dane, Greyhound mix. And mom and dad said they would keep Koolah, our other "mutt," until we were settled. We had enough stuff to distribute to friends and family, extra to sell, and still our truck was packed airtight.

Mom said, "A mosquito couldn't fit in there."

I know Amy was sad to see us go, but down deep I think she was thrilled to have a dog in the house again. Koolah is a dog that loves everyone. She greets people by smothering them with kisses from a tongue that moves as fast as a lizard's. Each lick covers your face from top to bottom and her tongue doesn't stop. The motion continues past your cheek and finishes with her tongue slapping the top of her nose. And Amy would let her "clean" her entire face. The fact that Koolah's breath is often described as "dragon's breath" didn't bother her either. Once again, she had a dog that would do anything for her, and loved every minute of it. Needless to say, Amy and Koolah doted on each other's love and affection. Amy had a shadow, and so did Koolah for that matter.

Like many dogs, Koolah knows when you are home before the door is opened. The only time you didn't get kisses from her was when she decided to say "hello" instead. Her hellos sound a little more like "woo-woo," because her mouth is *full*. She will grab whatever she can find, usually your slipper, a sock or a dog toy and hold it in her mouth as she parades around in front of you. She wriggles and wags her entire body. The benefit to this greeting is the fact that there is something in her mouth and therefore she cannot lick and kiss you all over. I must admit I prefer this greeting to the other.

Until this period in Koolah's life she was a farm dog. I still don't know exactly what her breeding is, but I think we've determined that she must have a herding dog in her heritage due to her instincts. She spent her days doing the barn chores with me. She knew our routine and had it down to a science as many herding dogs do. She knew where the horses went and what they should and should not do. For example, at feeding time she knew the horses were to "get back" from the stall door so I could give them their hay. If they didn't move back before the door was opened, she was nipping at their ankles as soon as she could get at them. And if the horses were impatient or bored and pawed at the ground, she was right there "barking" out orders.

I don't know whether Koolah longed for a different lifestyle or if she just wanted to be by Amy's side but my farm dog turned "soft" somewhere along the way. The dog that worked the horses, swam in the pond, and used a snow bank as a place to curl up for a nap, suddenly had a couch of her own, and a buddy to sleep with at night, one who didn't mind sharing her pillow and blanket. They went to the park together and played together, even ate together. That may be why the trim, fit farm dog went from 50 pounds to a plump 75 in less than 9 months.

I always knew she was a smart dog. She knew all the basic doggie tricks. She almost seemed to get bored with the usual, "sit, lie down, and gimmie five!"

Perhaps because she seemed so occupied with all the farm stuff, I didn't bother to teach her anything fancy. With that in mind, and the fact that Amy seemed to be able to get animals to do just about anything, I guess I wasn't surprised when my parents told me Koolah had added a few tricks to her book. Amy taught her to roll over and jump through hoops. This just proves the fact that with a little time and a lot of love, animals will do anything for their friends. And there was no doubt in anyone's mind that Koolah and Amy were the best of friends.

CHAPTER THIRTY-SEVEN
LONG DISTANCE RELATIONSHIP

Jimmy and I had picked up and transported all that we could fit into the back of our truck. We left very little room for ourselves. We spent our last weekend in Canada at our friends' place. Dan and Brenda graciously opened their doors on many occasions to their beautiful, large home, which to most was a little getaway on a lake near Haliburton, Ontario.

The weekend we left, our family threw a surprise 40th birthday party for my uncle Mark. It was actually a birthday party/going away party. As usual, the house was packed. We ate, drank, played cards and horseshoes, water-skied, etc., etc., etc....and at the end of the day we found a spot to sleep, if you were lucky, in a bed, sleeping bag, or on a mattress on the floor. On Saturday morning we had a huge brunch and started all over again. It was a great party weekend to celebrate my uncle's birthday and to send us off on our trip to Texas.

Sunday came quickly, as it always does, especially when you are having a good time. And it comes even quicker when you are about to leave loved ones behind. The morning we left my family formed a line of unhappy faces to say goodbye. It had to be one of the hardest things we have had to do in our lives. We went through the line one by one, exchanging goodbye hugs, kisses and tears. As we pulled away the line never broke. Everyone stood waving until we were out of sight.

It was a long trip, but the closer we got to Texas the more excited we became to see Jimmy's family. On Tuesday evening at nine o'clock we pulled into Jimmy's sister's place in Pflugerville, Texas, just north of Austin. It was a happy reunion for Jimmy and his family and I was finally going to meet the rest of my in-laws. His sister, Tammy, and his mom, Evelyn, greeted us at the door with open arms, hugs and kisses, even balloons, and suddenly the fact that I had left a family behind wasn't hurting quite so much.

We stayed with Tammy for a short while until we got on our feet and found a place to stay that would be suitable for our needs. The biggest factor in finding an apartment was a place that would accept dogs. It didn't take long. We found a one-bedroom apartment in the south end of Austin and large dogs were acceptable. I couldn't imagine finding a place that didn't take dogs. We would have to move again once we got Koolah there. And we all know how much I "love" moving.

Being a Canadian citizen, I was unable to work right away. We had been told the paperwork would only take a couple of days due to the fact that I was married to a U.S. citizen. Boy, were we misinformed! I spent eight long months unable to work while waiting for my work visa. So, needless to say, I was bored to tears during the day. The house stayed clean and dinner was always ready for Jimmy the moment he got in the door from work. But this was not what I was accustomed to. I wanted stalls to muck, horses to ride, and people to teach and interact with. My lifestyle had changed drastically. I had gone from a job that required me to be outdoors in the country, and on the go for the better part of the day and then some, to sitting in an apartment, in a big city where I knew very few people. So, when I talked to my family on the phone it was difficult to say the least. I missed them terribly. I missed my dog, too. Regardless of the fact that she was entertaining Amy, I wanted company.

When the phone rang in the middle of the day I had a pretty good guess as to who it might be. There was only one other person that would be home during the middle of the day, Amy. I guess she was bored, too. She had watched my parents use the speed dial button and directory enough times to figure it out all by herself.

When I answered the phone she always said, "Hello Deanne" with her most enthusiastic voice. I enjoyed our little chats about the weather, what we were doing, and Amy loved to tell me all the things she was doing with Koolah, which included asking Koolah to speak for me. She loved to do that one.
I hated to end our conversation but I knew she was home alone, and long distance calls during the day tended to be a little expensive.

I always asked her, "Amy, did you ask Mom if you could call me?"

Of course she would say yes.

I always told her, "I'm glad you asked Mom, because it costs money to call me in Texas."

Then I would ask her, who was going to pay for the phone call? Silence always fell on the other end of the phone when I asked this question. I knew she understood. I would have talked to her for hours. It seemed to help both of us through the days at home alone, but Mom's phone bill would have gone through the roof.

CHAPTER THIRTY-EIGHT
WEDDINGS

Most people enjoy weddings, some tolerate them, and others just go to "make an appearance." Amy, on the other hand, looked forward to a wedding with as much anticipation as if it were her own. She loved to see people dressed up, in love, dancing, and celebrating. She attended both of my weddings, and several of my cousins' weddings. She always had a little something special to add to each, with that "Amy touch."

My cousin Dave was the first to marry. Amy adored Dave, as a big cousin, and possibly a little more. He always saved a dance for her. He is the oldest of the cousins on the Tucker side, and for those of us who didn't have an older brother, he was the next best thing.

Jimmy and I were the next to join in marriage, and we exchanged vows twice. Amy made sure we knew how happy she was with our decision and told me how proud she was of me. At our bigger reception, she marched up to the microphone totally impromptu and announced to everyone how beautiful I was, and that she loved her Grandmas and me. No one had thought to ask her if she would like to say something. She saw others toasting the wedding party and felt she needed to do the same. It was short, sweet and very to the point. And for some reason she thought she should remind our grandmas that she loved them too.

Next in the lineup were Cindy and Joe. Amy had a soft spot for Joe and he seemed to keep her glowing whenever we got together. She had no problems telling Cindy she had a crush on her fiancé and that she was okay with them getting married. After the ceremony, Cindy sang a song to Joe. Amy thought she would do the same. She played her own beat on the drums and sang a little song in her own words. And once again, it was without a doubt, a second thought, or a moment's hesitation. She had no fear and loved to entertain.

Our cousin Melanie was the next to tie the knot. She has been

Our family at Cindy's wedding, including Jimmy on left.

more than a cousin to both Amy and me. We have shared dolls, secrets, clothes, makeup, and good times and bad, you name it, Melanie was always there. We are close in age, and lived close when we were young. And for Amy, she has been a friend who helped her see and do more things then any child could imagine. She helped Amy see that even though she may be "handicapped," she didn't have to have limitations. They traveled together, camped together, sang together, and most of all, laughed together. This is why Amy was chosen by Melanie and her husband Denis to do a very important job on their wedding day. She was the flower girl and the ring bearer, and she took her job very seriously.

Amy could hardly wait to get up to the microphone. She held her arm up high after every speaker, waving it anxiously in hopes that it was her turn next. When Amy stepped up to the microphone, the room was quiet. Everyone wanted to hear what she had to say to

Melanie. We all knew her speeches were becoming famous. They were genuine, truthful and straight from the heart. And because it was Melanie's wedding, perhaps we expected a heartfelt, touching, probably tear-jerking speech from Amy. Once again, her speech was short and sweet. She told Melanie she was proud of her and that she loved her. And to finish off her sweet "toast" to her best friend Mel, she told her that she thought she looked "like a princess."

Amy and Melanie on Melanie's Wedding Day

PART THREE
THE SUMMER OF 1997

⌘ ⌘ ⌘ ⌘

CHAPTER THIRTY-NINE
SLOWPOKE

In July of '97 we attended another wedding. My cousin Heather had met a guy named Gary while living in Hong Kong. Gary is originally from Leeds. So, much like our relationship, two nationalities joined together in holy matrimony. Jimmy was from Texas, and I was from Canada. Gary was from the U.K. and Heather was from Canada. It seemed there were guests from all four corners of the world. Jimmy and I were fortunate enough to find some reasonably priced tickets to fly home from Texas for the occasion. It was the first time I had been back to Canada since we had left the summer before.

On the day of the wedding, Amy was her usual, happy self. She had her turn at the microphone, entertained and socialized with everyone and danced the night away. The day after the wedding we made a trip to Niagara Falls with Heather, Gary and friends and family members who were visiting and hadn't seen "The Falls." It was a long walk from the parking lot to all the attractions. We checked out the casino and rode the Maid-of-the-Mist ferry that gives you an up-close view of the falls from below. We walked the strip that to many resembles a mini-Las Vegas, in Canada.

It was a long day for all of us, but Amy seemed to be dragging her feet the most. She just couldn't seem to keep up with the rest of us. Several times we found ourselves stopping to wait for her to catch up. She complained of being tired and we joked with her, not knowing what lie ahead. We teased her and called her slowpoke as we slowly made our way back to the car.

The trip back to Peterborough was long. I was happy that Mom said she would do the driving. Amy was asleep before we got on the highway and she slept the entire time. As much as I hate to admit it, I slept, too. We were exhausted. We had been on the go since the day we had arrived from Texas. We crammed in visits, shopping, partying, and site seeing into a small amount of time.

Before we knew it, our visit was over and we were standing outside the airport saying our goodbyes. Amy had made the trip to Toronto to see us off.

We exchanged a big, long hug, she added her little extra "lift" and said, "I'll miss you Deanne. I love you."

I told her, "I'll talk to you on the phone. And in the spring you're going to fly on a plane with Mom and Dad and come visit us in Texas."

She winked and said with a smile, "Wonderful."

CHAPTER FORTY
SLEEPYHEAD

Things got back to normal for everyone but Amy. She hadn't been herself since that day in Niagara Falls. She called Mom at work and told her she was sick. She was by herself so Mom went home to check on her. She had been sick so many times through her life, but never complained. She usually maintained her humor, and continued with her antics and pranks. Nothing seemed to slow her down. But when Mom got home, she found Amy sitting on the front porch crying. She took her inside, got her settled on the couch, propped her up with some pillows, and covered her with some blankets. Then she returned to work.

Before the week came to an end, she still seemed to be "under the weather." They were concerned that this may be more than a common cold. My parents took her to the clinic and they were told her chest was clear. She had a temperature but pneumonia was ruled out. When the weekend arrived she couldn't seem to get enough sleep. Even after Uncle Tom arrived, she fought to keep her eyes open while sitting at the table. She couldn't stand the thought of missing anything and insisted on sitting with everyone and trying her best to join in the fun. She fell asleep in her chair. Kym and Ian had been there earlier and suggested taking Amy to the hospital. After watching her fall asleep at the table knowing this was totally out of character for her, Mom decided to take her up to the emergency room.

After checking in a nurse took Amy into a screening room to check her vitals. She hooked her up to a pulseoximeter, a machine used to measure the oxygen levels in the blood. She was shocked to see how low the reading was. She thought it wasn't working because it was such a low reading. Mom reiterated how sick Amy had been and asked if she was sure it was reading correctly. The nurse told Mom if it was that low, she would be unconscious. She sent them back to the waiting room and went to find a doctor.

The doctor that examined her said she was definitely a sick young lady and felt it was necessary to admit her right away and put her on oxygen on the chance that the reading was correct. The only ward that had room for her was pediatrics. She was twenty-one years old.

The next morning Amy made her way to the bathroom. The short walk to the bathroom seemed to totally wear her out. She was so tired from walking that she shuffled her feet and drug her IV slowly beside her. The doctors then decided they should move her to Intensive Care. They tried some more medications and did a thoracentesis, a procedure that involves inserting a needle through her back to withdraw fluid off her lungs. They withdrew almost two liters. Amy sat on the edge of the bed and, as sick as she was, she maintained her good spirits and joked around with and teased the nurses.

After withdrawing the fluids, the doctor called my parents into a room to explain the severity of her situation. They were told it was possible that Amy could die. They returned to her room. My parents had seen Amy through so many things, including several cases of pneumonia. She looked very sick. Mom sat beside her and started to cry. She told Amy she needed to fight this. She had done it before and they refused to believe that she wouldn't make it through this.

I think the only time we saw my mother cry was the day my grandfather died. It brought such pain to each of us but Amy seemed to be affected the most. She couldn't stand to see anyone upset and to see my mother cry at her bedside must have upset her more than I could ever imagine. But this time she didn't have something clever to say. She looked at my mother, and her tears rolled down her cheeks.

CHAPTER FORTY-ONE
HAPPY BIRTHDAY AMY

Mom and Dad went to get something to eat. When they returned, they were delightfully surprised to see a dramatic difference with Amy. She was sitting up in her bed looking much better.

When Mom sat down Amy looked at her and said, "I'm not in Heaven anymore Mom."

Needless to say, this statement astonished Mom, and what she said next left her speechless. She told mom that she had seen Dianne's mother, Yvonne. She had passed away eight months earlier.

Amy pointed to her hand and said, "I saw her mom, and I saw her IV."

Amy knew she had died, but she did not know that before she passed she was in the hospital and she did in fact have an IV.

They had moved her to a spot where she could see down the hall.

When she saw Melanie nearing the door she said, "What the hell are you doing here?"

Her demeanor had changed so drastically. The last message friends and family members had received seemed so grim. They arrived expecting to see Amy barely hanging on.

But instead she belted out statements as if to say, "Why do you look so sad? I'm fine."

With things looking so positive, my parents went home to celebrate. Dad was telling everyone that she was going to be fine. He even announced her "recovery" off the front porch to anyone that would listen. My mother was happy but in the back of her mind she couldn't help but think it was too soon to celebrate; she may not be "out of the woods" yet.

At midnight my parents received a phone call from the hospital. Amy had had another downfall; they wanted to put her on a respirator. They needed my parents to come up to the hospital to sign some forms. After the respirator was hooked up, she seemed her perky self again, despite the fact that she was unable to talk. The doctors seemed very pessimistic and continued to tell my parents there was a strong possibility that she could die. Despite all of their warnings, my parents remained confident that she was going to pull through. They told the doctor's she had been sick before.

"She's going to make it," they said.

On August 20, 1997, Amy celebrated her 22nd birthday. Like many, she enjoyed her birthdays; they always meant cake, presents and a party with friends and family. And that's exactly what she got. Her birthday falls two days after Melanie's, so they always celebrated their birthdays together. Melanie came, and they celebrated. Melanie even painted Amy's fingernails and toenails for the occasion. She had several visitors that day, and they all came bearing gifts. And although she was on the respirator and had to stay in her bed, she still found ways to join in the fun and entertain as she always did.

The staff raised her bed to a sitting position and propped her up with pillows. She didn't want to miss anything and she rarely did. It seemed her only disappointment that day was the fact that she didn't get the movie she had asked for. Amy was a huge "Free Willy" fan. The movie "Free Willy 3" was about to be released in theaters and therefore not yet available in stores – the one gift that she had counted on the most and she couldn't have it.

I called the hospital to wish her a happy birthday. It was a difficult conversation; actually it wasn't a conversation at all. There was no voice on the other end of the line. I spoke and Amy listened. When Mom handed her the phone I sang "Happy Birthday" to her and tried to get Koolah to talk for her the way she used to for me. I knew she missed her. I could tell from the commotion on the other end of the line that the room was full of people. I wanted to be there, desperately.

As I spoke I could hear Mom in the background saying, "She's smiling. She's trying to laugh. Now she's crying! Okay, she's smiling again."

I knew she missed me as much as I missed her. Perhaps she missed Koolah even more. I told her I loved her and missed her and to get better so she could come visit me.

CHAPTER FORTY-TWO
DOUBLE TROUBLE

Throughout all of this, I was back in Texas. And trouble was just around the corner for me, too. I had discovered a lump behind my right ear. The Ear Nose and Throat Specialist that I saw felt it was necessary to remove it, as soon as possible. The MRI and CAT scan reports had stated that it was more than likely a benign tumor, but there wouldn't be a definite answer until it was removed and sent to a pathologist. I was torn. I had been on the phone with my parents, sometimes several times a day, getting reports on Amy's health. I can't imagine the strain my parents felt watching their youngest daughter's health rise and fall like a roller coaster, along with their emotions. And their eldest daughter was about to undergo approximately four hours of surgery to remove a lump in her parotid gland, not knowing if it was malignant or benign.

I wanted to come home in the worst way. Every time I spoke to my parents I wanted to be there for them and for Amy. I wished with all my heart I could make it go away. Mom and Dad agreed that I should stay in Austin and have the surgery done. Skipping it wasn't an option. They still believed Amy would be okay and there was no point in postponing my surgery to make a trip for nothing.

I remember dad saying, "Bite your lip and be strong. Take care of yourself first. She's going to be okay."

On August 28th I was admitted to the hospital and the surgery was performed. It was my first major surgery. For as much as I needed to concentrate on myself, I couldn't help but think of Amy. I worried about her more than myself. I sometimes wonder if I even realized how serious my situation was because I was so preoccupied with thoughts of Amy. I would tell myself that she has been through situations like this several times. She always bounced back. The nurses in her recovery room always commented on her sense of humor and positive and energetic attitude after surgery.

I remember being in the recovery room and hearing the nurse say, "Deanne, keep breathing, Deanne."

I made it through the surgery but couldn't live up to my sister's perky personality while in recovery. I was still a little out of it when they wheeled me back to my room. All that stuck in my mind was the fact that the doctor said the pathology report was back already and it was benign. The tumor turned out to be the size of a golf ball. And the surgery had left the right side of my face partially paralyzed. My doctor explained that this would be temporary.

The doctors in Peterborough told my parents there was nothing more they could do for Amy. They felt she had a 50/50 chance of surviving. They decided to transfer her to the hospital in Kingston, Ontario. There were specialists there along with a well-known university that could possibly shed some light on Amy's illness.

My father couldn't sleep and went to the hospital in the middle of the night to visit her. Amy was resting so he stood in the hallway talking to one of the nurses.

In mid-conversation the nurse said, "Look at this."

His back was facing the window to Amy's room. He turned around to see her throw one of her teddy bears in his direction. She knew he was there to visit her, and she demanded his attention. Dad sat and visited with her. He told her she was going to go to another hospital in a helicopter. She looked at him and gave the "thumbs up."

August 29th is my parents' anniversary. Late that evening, the paramedics came to pick Amy up for the trip to Kingston General. When they came to her room, she pointed to all of her machines to make sure they didn't forget anything. Once everything was loaded, including Amy and her entourage, Mom and Dad stood in front of the hospital and watched the helicopter take off.

As they flew off Mom thought to herself, "This could be the beginning of the end."

Though they may not admit it out loud, I'm sure this thought crosses many parents' minds when their child is extremely ill, and when doctors say things like, "There's nothing more we can do for her" or, "There is a strong possibility that your child may not make it through this."

With everything in your heart you want to believe differently, and for as much as you may think you are prepared for the worst-case scenario, you never are.

CHAPTER FORTY-THREE
GETTING SETTLED IN KINGSTON

Mom and Dad got some sleep and headed for Kingston early the next morning. When they arrived the intensive care unit said they were not sure why they brought Amy there. As the testing continued their questions ceased and they began to realize just how sick Amy really was. Her oxygen levels were constantly up and down and they were never within the "normal" range.

Throughout all of this, Amy's concerns were focused on the patient across the hall from her. He had been in a car accident and was in a coma. She repeatedly asked about him, pointing to the room and making gestures. Her situation was never more important. She always put others ahead of herself.

We have several relatives living in the city of Kingston. My mother's cousin, Arlene graciously offered her home to my family.

She and her son Eric opened their doors and said, "Stay as long as you need."

Mom had to go back to work. Dianne and Brenda Whalen, both being nurses, offered their professional advice and honest opinions as friends. They both felt Mom should stay. Brenda warned them of the risks of being on the respirator for a long period of time.

She told them, "The longer she is on the respirator the less chance she has for survival."

They were told she had developed a 'syndrome' known as A.R.D.S. (Adult Respiratory Distress Syndrome). Her chances for survival had dropped. Statistics stated that her chances had dropped from 50/50 to 40 percent. She had spiked a high temperature, which indicated more infection, and she continued to sleep a lot. But the doctors said Amy was stable. So, on Sunday evening Mom returned to Peterborough to go back to work and Dad stayed in Kingston.

Dad used Eric's bike to travel back and forth from the hospital, and Amy continued to be in good spirits. Her room was filled with pictures and a couple of her teddy bears from her birthday party. Dad played catch with her teddy bears and did all he could to keep her busy. And the staff was kind enough to allow a tape recorder in her room. So music played constantly for her, including a tape that Melanie and Denis made especially for her to help keep her room cheerful. A positive attitude was imperative in my Dad's eyes. There was no alternative.

On Wednesday, Dianne and Brenda's brother, Father Richard Whalen came to visit Amy. Another friend of the family, Ted, came to visit also. He brought a picture of his dog, Earl and Koolah. As Father Richard talked to her he noticed the picture of Koolah and Earl. He told Amy how much he liked dogs and said he would like to have one. Amy shook her head as if to say, "you can't have those dogs." She knew they both had homes and she wasn't about to let Father Richard think he could have either of them. Even though that was not the thought behind his statement, "I would like to have one," Amy didn't even give him a chance to ask.

Amy had visitors on a regular basis. If it wasn't a family member, it was a specialist, nurse or an intern. Every morning there was a meeting and consultations regarding Amy's current condition. There were so many people present it seemed half of the hospital was there to participate or possibly find a solution to her health problems. The option of "re-traching" her was brought up. They were doing everything they could to try to get her oxygen levels close to or back to normal, as the medications weren't helping.

On Thursday morning Amy went into a terrible coughing spell. The staff asked my father to leave the room as they couldn't seem to get it under control. So Dad took the opportunity to go down to the cafeteria and get a coffee. When he returned, he was told they had to put her under because she was coughing and gagging so violently. Dad's first thought was that he was robbed of his last chance to say anything to her. Whenever changes were made with Amy's health or condition, Mom or Dad always took the time to explain to her what was about to happen. She always had the opportunity to let us know she was okay with whatever procedure was about to be performed. It was usually her famous "thumbs-up" sign.

But this time, he never got the chance. He walked into her room to find her sleeping, unable to wake her to tell her everything was going to be okay. Dad called Mom, but didn't explain the whole situation to her. He didn't want her to drive to Kingston like a mad woman. Aunt June had said she would work for Mom. So Mom was on her way.

As she drove, she knew something wasn't right. Things just seemed to be getting worse with each passing day. What she didn't know was that when she arrived at the hospital she was going to see Amy in a comatose state.

A specialist came in to speak to Mom and Dad on Friday morning. He had consulted with doctors from Amy's past, including the doctors from Sick Kids in Toronto. They were still contemplating the thought of giving her another trache. They needed to find a way to get more oxygen into her system. All the machines and medications just didn't seem to be enough.

Things seemed to be deteriorating for Amy. Her levels continued to jump up and down, but the highest number of the day was decreasing with every day that passed. While she was awake her levels would drop from the small effort that was needed to turn her on to her side. Now she was motionless and there was still no improvement.

CHAPTER FORTY-FOUR
TIME TO GO HOME

On Saturday morning I had to be at work at 6:30. I had only been back to work a couple of days. I had been talking to my parents two, sometimes three times a day. For some reason, it was different that morning. When I spoke to my parents I could tell things were getting worse. In the back of my mind I had the sinking feeling that they were beginning to hear the doctors' words of warning. I needed to go home.

I called Jimmy and asked him to find tickets for us as soon as possible. He understood that we needed to go home, but he and my parents had one condition. I had to clear flying with my doctor. It had been only eight days since my surgery. My doctor was off for the day. I put a page in to the doctor on-call. He called me back within minutes. After explaining my surgery and the situation he told me it would be okay to fly. My only instructions were to take an antihistamine and some chewing gum. Jimmy found us some tickets leaving that day direct from Dallas to Toronto. I went home and packed enough stuff to get us through the weekend. We were out the door and on I-35 headed north before noon.

The drive to Dallas was stressful. We were pushing our time limit. Half of the time we worried about Amy and the other half we worried we would miss our plane. We arrived within an hour of our departure time. We still had to park the truck, shuttle to the airport, check-in, etc. If you have ever been to the airport in Dallas, you would understand our severe lack of time to do all of the above. We got inside and after checking in, ran straight to our gate.

As we boarded we heard the flight attendant announcing, "The Sheads are here."

Our flight went smoothly, but we hit a dead-end when we arrived. Mom had called ahead to reserve a rental car for us. All of our friends and family members who lived in the Toronto area were already in

Kingston or on their way. The company had made all the arrangements and taken Mom's credit card number, but when we got to the counter, they said they could not rent a vehicle to us. Their policy stated, "The renter must match the name on the credit card." After telling the customer service representative that this had been pre-arranged and already approved, she refused to rent the vehicle to us. We then proceeded to explain the situation to her. But it didn't matter that my sister was extremely ill and that we had flown in from Texas and needed transportation to Kingston immediately.

I didn't have room on my card for her to swipe the $500 deposit. We had just purchased our plane tickets with it. I made several phone calls to my mother, and she too made many calls to the rental company, their head office and then to another company, one who could look beyond their policy to help someone in need. We shuttled to their office, filled out the necessary paperwork and were on our way to Kingston. Only three hours left on our journey to see Amy.

On the way there, I struggled with the thought, "should I go directly to the hospital to see her or should I wait 'til the morning?"

I was worried about how I would react seeing her lying there not able to wake her to see her beautiful smile. If I went to her room, I could peek in on her, imagine her sleeping, and then go home with a vision that may have been easier to handle. I had been told of all the equipment, the respirator tubes, the tape and her swollen tongue. She had marks on her hands, ankles, thighs and neck. They had all been used for the IV. I tried to envision her room, the pictures, the music, and her resting comfortably, and rather than "disturbing her," I decided to go straight to Arlene's to be with the rest of the family.

We pulled up to Arlene's late on Saturday night. The house was full of family and friends. We sat around the small kitchen table and talked 'til the wee hours of the morning. Our conversations circled around my surgery and Amy. Those who had seen her awake spoke of her antics, pranks and constant entertaining. The rest of us remembered her healthy and active, we shared our thoughts and special memories of days gone by.

Laughing was difficult for me. My surgery had left me with a droopy smile. I self-consciously held my hand in front of my lips every time someone tried to make me smile or laugh. If anyone caught a glimpse of my crooked lips, the laughter would double. It was therapy for everyone in the room. And despite the fact that things were looking grim to many, my parents insisted we think positive. Amy needed us to think positive, and quite frankly we did, too. We couldn't imagine life without her.

CHAPTER FORTY-FIVE
DEEP SLEEP LULLABIES

I woke up Sunday morning to the smell of fresh coffee brewing and the sound of familiar voices. I could hear my parents talking in the kitchen. I went downstairs to pour myself a cup and join in the conversation. As I made my way down the stairs, I took the time to look at all of Arlene's paintings. I thought to myself how great it felt to be "home." I just wished it was for a happier occasion. We talked about everything that had happened, mostly to refresh my memory, and to discuss every possible reason for Amy's situation, searching desperately for a solution.

It was evident that there was an infection present, but where had it come from? Mom told me they had even done a pelvic exam, thinking it may be possible that she was experiencing "toxic shock syndrome." Mom was grasping at strings and it was a long shot, but she had to be sure they had explored every option. The exam revealed nothing but normal results.

After breakfast and a pot or two of coffee, we piled into the car and headed over to the hospital. I realized I only had a short distance to "prep" myself for what I was about to see. Images flashed through my mind – the machines, monitors, tubes and room where my sister lay quietly was about to be a reality, and I would be lying if I said I was "okay" with what I was about to see. Perhaps I was trying to make the situation easier for me. What made it difficult was the fact that the face I knew so well, the face that always had a smile that made fears and doubts for so many disappear, would be expressionless. The eyes that brightened the gloomiest of days were closed. And the giggle that warmed our hearts couldn't be heard.

I took a deep breath as we stepped off the elevator, and walked into the intensive care unit. As we passed the nurses' station, my parents gave us a brief introduction.

"This is the big sister, all the way from Texas."

As we approached her room, I felt the rush of anticipation and before I had the chance to worry about what I was about to see, I heard the music of an acoustic guitar and my cousin Melanie singing a familiar song. I became calm and collected, ready to be by my sister's side. I walked past the curtain to see Amy sleeping peacefully. The machines didn't bother me like I expected them to. I had seen her hooked up to many over the years. I walked to her bedside taking in all the photos and mementos on the windowsill, and listened to the small tape recorder in the corner that I was told played continuously for her. What made the tape special was the fact that Melanie and Amy sang some of the songs together, with some giggles in between. So the laughter I thought I wasn't going to hear was there after all.

I sat down on the chair beside her bed and picked up her lifeless hand to hold it in mine. I said hello and proceeded to tell her how I had got there and that Jimmy was with me. He stood quietly at the end of the bed. I told her all about our plane ride and the roadblocks we had experienced along the way, all to come to see her. And for as much as I hated to say it, I told her she needed to get better, because Jimmy and I could only stay 'til Tuesday, so "fight this battle like all the others, and get better."

I jokingly told her how everyone was going to so much trouble for her and I hoped she was enjoying all the attention, as usual. I had to tease her; if the tables were turned she would do the same to me. I wished I had the comedic lines and faces, the pranks that brought laughter and tears of joy, but I lacked that "Amy flair." The fun that always filled the room when she was present had gone the day she had to close her eyes.

We took turns at her side, talking to her, telling jokes. Kendra read to her and I sang lullabies, songs from our childhood, songs we still sing today whenever we're all together.

One of the nurses told my father, "You have a beautiful family."

She was amazed with the closeness and love that we shared and shared openly. Our support ran stronger than just a hand to hold or a shoulder to cry on. I have always been proud of my family, but never as proud as I was that week. Once again we were reminded of just how deep our family bond is. We were there for Amy and for each other. Our friends came from great distances to provide even more support, our extended family that is there whenever we need them. And through all of this the hospital was kind enough to let anyone in who came to visit Amy, family member or not.

As the hours passed we continued to pray and hope for a miracle, despite what some of the staff members had said. One of the nurses asked my mother if our family had discussed the possibility that Amy might not make it through this. He told my mother that we needed to prepare the family for the worst-case scenario. It was true we hadn't discussed it. The thought never crossed our minds. In the middle of the conversation my father came through the door. My mother didn't get the opportunity to respond to the nurse's questions. My father was adamant that things would change. In his mind there was no other option. He was the driving force behind us all. He refused to believe Amy was going to do anything but get better.

Angrily he told us, "We don't have to discuss it because it wasn't going to happen. She will make it through this."

Then he turned and left.

Later that evening, Mom and Dad took a walk down to the waterfront. They still didn't want to believe that she wasn't going to pull through. It was clear to many of us that the hopes of the staff were diminishing. Although we were told miracles can happen, the expressions on their faces led us to believe that a miracle is what we were looking for now. For as strong as Amy was, she couldn't do this on her own. She was too sick.

Mom told Dad, "Maybe this was how it was meant to be."

She told him that she had laid in bed many a night worrying, "What if one or both of us went first? How would she cope with a loss so great? Who would care for her? What would happen?"

If it *were* "Amy's time," she would never have to face such a terrible loss.

CHAPTER FORTY-SIX
TUESDAY

Another day had passed of lullabies, music, and books, and numbers that seemed to decrease with every hour. It was Tuesday morning. Jimmy and I were booked to go home, but the thought of leaving was unbearable. We spent the morning on the phone talking to the airlines, desperately looking for an extension that wasn't outrageously expensive on such short notice. The first representative we spoke to told us we would have to pay over $500 each for rescheduling fees. A supervisor told us it would be a little over $200 each. Though the amount was decreasing, these prices weren't what we wanted to hear. I had already taken so much time off work for my surgery.

We finally got through to a manager and she was more than helpful and sympathetic to our situation. All she needed to know was what hospital Amy was in, what ward she was in and her full name. After being on hold for several minutes she came back to the line and said I can extend your tickets for one more week for $50 total.

Graciously we accepted and before hanging up the phone she said, "I hope your sister will make a full recovery and God Bless you and your family."

I couldn't wait to get to the hospital to tell Amy. As I sat by her bedside telling her all that we had been through that morning a nurse came in to change her lines and IV bags. My attention was drawn to her as I watched the numbers on the monitor begin to fall. Normally the numbers would fluctuate back and forth, always keeping within a constant range. But once the lines had been disconnected they dropped steadily. I watched as the nurse calmly went on with her job, but couldn't help but worry as I saw the numbers dipping lower and lower. My story had ended long ago and I felt my heart rate increase and my breathing change as I silently watched what seemed like it may be the end for my sister.

The day before I had seen her numbers in the 50s and 60s and now they were plummeting into the low teens.

I fought back the urge to scream at the nurse, "Would you hurry the hell up!"

But before I exploded with anger the lines were up and running again with a full supply of medicine and fluids, and her numbers were climbing.

I took a deep breath and wondered if Amy had felt the same anguish I had felt. Did she feel anything? Did she understand what was happening? Throughout the whole ordeal she remained silent and still, as always. I hoped she was as peaceful on the inside as she looked on the outside. Hope was all we had to hang onto, and we had to hang on to something.

Our arrival at the hospital this morning was unlike any other. For the first time we seemed to understand that a miracle wasn't available and our hope had run out. We were told Amy had had a bad night. Her lungs had become what some doctors call "wet" and were unable to function properly anymore. No antibiotic could cure her condition, and she wasn't a good candidate for a transplant. The words "it's only a matter of time" struck deep into our hearts, and our world would be changed forever.

Before long the hospital was flooded with friends and family members. We packed into her small corner in the intensive care unit taking turns watching her sleep peacefully, holding her hand, and telling her how much we loved her. There were times when Amy appeared to be opening her eyes. Many of us, refusing to believe these were her last moments, pleaded with her to wake up, open her eyes and fight this with all her might. When we told the nurses we had seen her eyes opening, regretfully they explained that in her condition, it is possible that she is opening her eyes but only in reaction to the seizures she may be experiencing due to the lack of oxygen in her system. There was enough medication in her system to keep even a healthy person in a very deep sleep.

My family and I sat in the chapel with Father Whalen. We sat in a small circle talking about Amy. We talked about her life. What she had done and how she had touched so many people in her "angelic" ways. She had left an imprint on the heart of everyone she met. Her attitude toward life was clear; live each day to the fullest, which she did. She never had regrets, held grudges, or worried about tomorrow. Each day was a day worth treasuring. We wondered if she knew her time on earth would be short. It may explain why she lived the way she did, did the things she did and loved as openly as she did.

Jokingly Father Whalen said, "If she doesn't make it into Heaven, there isn't much hope for the rest of us."

As the day wore on, my parents struggled with the thought of saying goodbye to Amy. There was someone at every inch of Amy's bedside; someone was always holding her hand. As evening fell, my parents could no longer bear the thought of watching her take her last breaths as they stood by helplessly. For them, it wasn't Amy anymore, just the machines that kept taking in air to the lungs that couldn't keep a supply of oxygen for the rest of her body. I watched through a blur of tears as my parents turned to leave the room. I fought the urge to stay and couldn't decide where I wanted to be most – with my mom and dad or by my sister's side. I took another look at her and tried to force out the word "goodbye" with a kiss.

Before leaving her room I asked friends and family members to stay with her. I asked them to hold her hand, tell her we still loved her and that we were sorry we couldn't stay. I just wanted someone to be there for her. The thought of her being alone in her final hours seemed to hurt more than saying goodbye did. Everyone I spoke to agreed to stay by her side. So I left knowing she wouldn't leave this world alone. I never looked back. We met Mom and Dad at the car and drove back in silence to Arlene's house.

When we arrived there was still a houseful of people waiting to be there for our family, for each other. My dad picked up his guitar and started to play. Again, our family exchanged favorite "Amy stories" and slowly the smiles reappeared.

Mom hugged me and said, "We're not crying for Amy, we're crying for ourselves."

I wished I could look at it that way. Instead I sat in the living room feeling guilty that I wasn't there for her. I kept picturing her lying in the hospital bed with friends and family, but not one person from her immediate family there to say goodbye. It wasn't right.

I turned to Jimmy and said, "I have to go, I have to be there for her."

When we got to the hospital, my cousin David met us at the elevator. The look on his face told me we were too late.

He struggled with the words, "She's gone," and we stood in the doorway of the elevator holding each other, crying together over our tremendous loss. We knew our family would never be the same.

I forced myself to stay on the elevator. Even though it was too late, I had to say goodbye one more time. I would never forgive myself if I didn't. The elevator door opened on the floor for the intensive care unit and I was surrounded by more family members with another flood of tears and hugs. In all the commotion I hadn't noticed that Jimmy had disappeared.

He came through the doors and whisked me away from the grievances whispering, "She's not gone yet. The nurse said you can come say goodbye."

The room was quiet, and dim. The only light in the room was the glow from her monitors and machines. For the first time I was able to look at her knowing she was at peace. I clutched her hand and held it to her chest.

As her heart pumped for the last time, I leaned over and kissed her forehead whispering, "Goodbye my sweet angel. Say hello to Granddad and Molson for me."

And the room went dark.

My most vivid memories from Amy's funeral are as follows: sitting in the church listening to music by her favorite singer, from the movie *Free Willy*, one of her favorite movies. The music seemed to lift our spirits to the highest steeple despite our incredible loss. And my favorite memory was Father Whalen pointing out Amy's full name, Amy Ninette. He told us the true meaning behind each of her names. Amy meant "beloved," and Ninette meant "little dear." And that's exactly what she was, a *beloved little dear* to everyone she met. She will live in our hearts forever.

In Loving Memory of Amy Ninette Tucker
August 20, 1975 – September 10, 1997

EPILOGUE

Although Amy is no longer with us, her presence in Peterborough will never be forgotten. An Amy Tucker Memorial Award was established at Saint Peter's High School. My parents have gone every year to present the award to the deserving graduating student.

Two seats were purchased at Showplace Theatre by friends and family. Amy's name has also been put in the Butterfly Garden, which was established in Peterborough to honor the memory of children who passed away leaving a permanent mark on all those who knew them. Both of these "tributes" to Amy were organized by our aunt June Woodside.

Throughout the days of Amy's wake and funeral one bright star remained in the sky all by itself, and we believe it was her telling us she was okay and her suffering was over.

As my mother has said: "She loved life and people so much that she would not have been happy continuing as an invalid. We all loved her and gave her as much opportunity as possible to grow and develop to the best of her ability. She did that and more. Thank you, Amy, for being a part of our lives."

The following entries were also put into a book made by my cousin Melanie, which she presented to my parents shortly after Amy passed away.

Inscription at Showplace Theatre by Melanie Keyes

Amy didn't often discuss her philosophy of life but demonstrated her ideals through her actions with ingenious simplicity.
Amy woke at dawn to eagerly meet the day, and would catch naps when she was tired. She indulged in the things she loved and savored each precious moment.
Amy loved to laugh with others. She never focused on her own

limitations, but always recognized and offered a hand to those in need.

Amy hugged a lot. She avoided pretense and abandoned shyness. Amy took pride in herself. She had an inherent confidence that many would envy.

Amy loved animals, sports and children of all ages. Her sense of fun and excitement was natural and contagious.

Amy loved her family and her home. At the end of the day, no matter what the fun or festivities, she knew where she wanted to be.

We could all learn a lot about life from someone as special as Amy. These seats are for you, Amy, because we know you are watching.

"Sit beside me, and I'll always be your friend."

In the spring of 1998, a memorial seat was purchased at Showplace Theatre in honor of Amy. Her balcony seat is number 22 and reads *In Memory of Amy Tucker.*

Seat number 23 is inscribed with the words, *"Amy's friend."*

This short profile is included in a book in the foyer at Showplace Theatre.

Like a Precious Butterfly
by June Woodside

"Like a precious butterfly Amy flew into our lives. Since we heard those words, "It's a hat trick," as your daddy proudly gave us the news that you had arrived, we loved you. There you were, sitting in my flower bed, smiling and beautiful like a butterfly that had landed for a pausing moment.

You brought pleasure to all who knew you and you brought a special love to our family. It was our fortune to have you so close to us as you grew from a tiny baby to become a young lady. We were able to watch every step as you enjoyed learning new things. You were excited about each new experience and you never stopped making us laugh.

In more recent years, I recall the moments of you taking part in family weddings. From somewhere came the perfect words as you spontaneously held a microphone and toasted the brides and grooms. In your simple way, you could say just the right words that would touch our hearts deep inside.

In the past summer, you and I spent an afternoon sitting on a blanket in our backyard. We assembled a photo album as I put the pictures in and you held the pages. We laughed as we looked at the pictures of the family over the past year. You were amused as usual at the simple things and you thought I was funny because it hurt me to sit on the hard ground. Somehow it made the pain seem not so bad because you kept laughing as I whined. We moved the blanket all around the yard, trying to avoid the hot sun. Like a butterfly moving from place to place, flapping its wings, pausing to enjoy the day.

I know that you enjoyed the day as I did. I will enjoy that day in my mind forever. You will remain in my heart as a precious butterfly, and every time I see you flutter by, I'll say, "Hello Amy. I love you Amy, and I'm glad to see you in my garden again."

Mailed from Laredo, Texas
December, 1997

Pete: Amy was so independent and smart from an early age for a handicapped child; able to make herself understood; a prankster – sly looks and grins imitated. She knew even more than we gave her credit for. Every time she saw me she gave me the sign, "Fingers in nostrils" even as she learned to speak she pronounced "Pete"– "Peach" and it stuck!

I know how much she loved my dog Sam. Even though she was a little rough on him in the beginning– they became good buddies.

Lynn: Amy could create a situation with anything available (e.g. underwear over her ears for a Santa Claus beard. One time she walked into Mom's dining area– cap to one side, pipe in mouth, cane and limping looking like Poppa (How did she know?).

I recall the time she tried to hit the piñata and shouted, "Hold still you son of a bitch!" It was hilarious. Amy loved the water. Fits of coughing and aspiration of water could not stop her from swimming when she had a tracheotomy. She was always determined, persevering and enjoying life to the fullest. She later became a medal winner in swimming, cross-country skiing and shot-put. She did our family proud! We miss her more every day!

Ode to Amy
By Lynn Palmer

Two loving parents with the patience of Job,
Two older sisters to help share the load,
So many moments, much happiness to share,
With the Cassidys, the Tuckers, and many others who cared.
A heart full of love coming straight from within,
No inhibitions at all, just a contagious grin.
Her insights were amazing, her sign language, too,
Amy never missed a trick but she played lots on you.
A great sense of humor right 'til the end,
A wink, an expression, or maybe tickling your chin.
She taught us about courage in her own fearless way,
A heart like a lion, Special Olympics, and day after day
Enthusiasm, joy, such a fun-loving girl;
GOD loaned her to us, this rare little pearl!
Look up at night and you'll catch her twinkling eye,
She'll be a bright shining star sitting high in the sky.
Footprints on our hearts comfort each one,
Amy's memory will be forever, like warmth from the sun.

My Memory of Amy
by Angela Fisher

My memory of Amy is on the steps of Casa Loma. We were going into Gary and Heather's wedding. Amy looked at me and smiled that warm smile she always had for everyone and said, "Hi!"

I asked her if she remembered me and she hesitated, and honestly replied, "Well...um... not really." I said I was Denis' mom and she said, "Oh ya, Angela!" with a proud look that sticks in my mind and brings a smile to my face every time I think of it.

Grandma Helen Remembers:

I recall one time out at Mallard Bay. Nora and I were babysitting. Amy had been given a perm and at the back it had become extremely matted. She was not able to have anyone touch it. I said to Nora, "Let's cut her hair. If you can amuse her, I'll do the cutting." So out came a box of powder, rouge and all the make-up we could find. Amy powdered and painted Nora's face and I was able to get the hair untangled. Everyone had fun even though Nora looked like a ghost.

Amy

I am a sad girl who misses her cousin
I wonder if Amy went to Heaven
I hear her trying to talk to me in my sleep
I see her, but I can't touch her
I want to see Amy again
I am a sad girl who misses her cousin

I pretend talk to her when I am alone
I feel her hand comforting me when I am sad

I touch the teddy bear her parents gave me
that used to be hers
I worry that I will forget her
I cry when I think about the wonderful life she led
I am a sad girl who misses my cousin

I understand that I may not see her again until I die
I say she will be deeply missed by everyone
I dream that everything that happened is all a dream
I try to remember the good times
like Special Olympics
I hope she will open the gate for me when I die
I am a sad girl who misses her cousin.

Lisa Tucker
Cherished Cousin

From Cousin Heather

I remember so well when you were born. Another cousin! We were all so excited that Aunt Lois and Uncle Spencer had another baby. I remember all the adults teasing your dad about "another girl." At that point, I didn't know cousins came in boys. I also remember the day when my mom and dad told me that you were a little different than other babies. They tried to explain but I didn't really understand. I was seven.

Over the years, I did notice that you were different, but we just played with you and learned your ways. Always smiling and laughing, imitating, gesturing. You were just another one of the cousins.

I'm so glad we spent so much time together as kids. We all developed our own interests; yours were animals, E.T., and Michael Jackson. A very big part of your life was Mel. Your sing-song friend, dress up, fames, fun and smiles filled your time together. You're a very special friend. And luckily that brought you much closer to me.

Through all the times you came to spend with us, you shared your love with everyone. Thank you.

I saw you many times once I returned from Hong Kong. You were at every party. I noticed you had changed into a young woman. Independent and strong, you took care of yourself and other people.

When you took the microphone at my wedding, the guests were mesmerized. Here was a beautiful tribute to a dearly loved cousin. You understood what weddings were for– family and friends together, expressions of love. When you told me you were proud of us, you took my breath away. I'm so glad you shared our day.

Soon after that you were in the hospital. And as usual, your boundless spirit took hold. Even then you brought love into centre view. You pulled the family together, a family that had had some turbulence in the past. You performed the surgery that healed our family forever.

Looking forward is very difficult for all of us. To go on without you in our daily lives seems impossible at times. Looking back is much easier. Remembering all of the good times, the hugs and kisses and that unforgettable smile of yours. I know you're sharing it with others wherever you are now.

For Our Cousin and Special Friend
by Cindy Mazza

So sweet, yet so mischievous, always smiling, forever generous. You taught us all so very much, even though here such a short while, an angel to us all, touching our hearts with your smile.

I recall just a short time ago, speaking to a woman who had a Down Syndrome child and a family she knew who did. I told her with no doubt and with great pride how lucky they were to have an angel close by. I told her I believed these children are truly a gift and that God himself hand picks their parents. She paused momentarily smiled and nodded her head, "I do believe you are right, and thank you. I'll be sure to tell them what you have said." I left that lady with a warm feeling that day, then we took some time to remember you, Amy, as we often do, shedding a tear and missing you.

Your witty comments, your tenderness and your laugh. "Hello McFly!""Where's Joe?" "Joe, hit me!" Your messages to Joe on our answering machine, your love for him and your little love messages, always trying to sneak the seat beside him. Watching me sing to Joe at our wedding, you looking over his shoulder, never taking your eyes off me and being the first to hug me and say, "Good job. Love you!"

Always wanting to be in the middle of the excitement – Dad's 50th. "U Peach" the license plate and our dad's new nickname. Warm Hugs and Tender Touch! We miss you Amy! Thanks for blessing our lives!

Down Syndrome – The Third Parent
By Melanie Keyes

Amy was so much like Lois and Spencer in appearance and in character. I saw so much of each of them expressed in her. She also resembled her sisters in many ways.

I saw Down Syndrome in Amy as well, the way that you see that "family resemblance;" a glimmer of the parent in a child – the qualities, the traits, the mannerisms and appearance. In my mind, Down Syndrome was like a third parent. This became apparent to me when I worked with other people who had Down Syndrome. I would closely observe my other Down Syndrome friends, and would sometimes to my surprise, recognize things that I thought were uniquely Amy. A certain facial expression, a movement, an articulation… gifts from the third parent, a Down Syndrome trait.

I don't hate Down Syndrome for giving Amy the weak heart, lungs and respiratory system that failed her. I certainly do not hate Down Syndrome for the ways it made her different. It is actually to the contrary. I am grateful to Down Syndrome as I am to Spencer and Lois, for its contribution in bringing life to the perfect child.

My Memories
From Melanie Keyes

I paid such close attention to Amy. She had a presence, or perhaps we simply had a connection which drew in my attention. I am happy to say I can still watch her like a movie in my head. She imprinted herself so clearly on my life that I can hear her voice, see her face, watch her movements and feel her hug from where she stood beaming up into my face with her sparkling eyes.

I think it was much more than the amount of time we spent together, that left her so closely with me… it was a deeper awareness she brought to me. She made me feel awake and in tune. She was pure energy.

Words of Comfort
By Melanie Keyes

A friend of mine recently lost a brother. He had two daughters in their early 20s. The girls said they didn't ever want to "get over" the death of their father, because then who would they be? They were afraid that if they came to peace with so tragic a loss, certainly they will have forgotten who he was and how much they loved him.

As one who has been through the most intimate of tragedies, I have learned that losing the terrible shock that comes with death, in no way makes you lose the love or the wonderful memory of the person who has died. I was fearful at first that I would forget things about Amy (important, beautiful details), but this has in no way happened. She made too great an impression on my life.

I'll never be over the loss of Amy, but gradually, over time, I am more often able to think of her with a smile and gratitude than with tears and heartache. Amy continues to teach me so much about life.

Amy was charming and witty. My stories of her arise in response to any number of situations. And I am just one person who loved her. Together we can all share stories of Amy to last the rest of our lives.

Let the stories go on! Stories of Amy, for whom our love will continue to change and grow, as we come to realize her depth of character, the significance of her life on our souls, and the love she brought to our lives.

Love and a Million Thanks, Melanie

NOTES AND ACKNOWLEDGEMENTS

Showplace – Contact - Tammy Duncan
Address:
Showplace Peterborough
290 George St. North
Peterborough, ON K9J 3H2
705- 742-7089

Butterfly Garden – Contact - Nancy McLinden
Address:
Bereaved Families of Ontario Affiliate
187 Simcoe St.
Peterborough, ON K9H 2H6
   The garden is beside the Otonabee River on the Millennium Walkway and it is called "Our Children Remembered." It is a Butterfly Memorial Garden for parents to remember children that they have lost. (It is not for still births, but rather for children that have lived and died no matter what age).

Cover designed by Denis Keyes
Address:
1 High Park Gardens
Toronto, ON M6R 1S8

Key Music Therapy – Contact – Melanie Keyes
Address:
1 High Park Gardens
Toronto, ON M6R 1S8

Neitek Farms/Services – Contact – John Neill
Address:
2551 Heritage Line

Peterborough, ON K9J 6X8

Claireville Ranch – Contact – Barry Thomson
Address:
8742 Claireville
R R # 8 Brampton, ON L6T 3Y7

Many thanks to the staff at the three following hospitals for all their help over the years:

Peterborough Regional Health Centre
Address:
1 Hospital Drive
Peterborough, ON K9J 7C6

Kingston General Hospital
Address:
76 Stuart St.
Kingston, ON K7L 2V7

Toronto Hospital for Sick Children
Address:
555 University Ave.
Toronto, ON M5G 1X8

Peterborough & District Association For Community Living
Address:
223 Aylmer St.
Peterborough, ON K9J 3K3

Five Counties Children's Centre
Address:
872 Dutton St.
Peterborough, ON K9H 7G1

Special thanks to the Separate School Board of Peterborough for their support of integration.

Thank you to Deanna Martell, for being the first to proofread my story and give me an objective opinion, with constructive criticism.